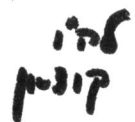

THE BOOK OF RUTH

MeAm Lo'ez

בצאת ישראל ממצרים בית יעקב
מעם לועז

The Book of Ruth

MeAm Lo'ez

by

Rabbi Shmuel Yerushalmi

Translated by
E. van Handel

Edited by
Dr. Zvi Faier

MAZNAIM PUBLISHING CORPORATION
NEW YORK / JERUSALEM

Copyright © 1985 by Maznaim Publishing Corporation

All rights reserved. This book, or parts thereof, may not be reproduced in any form without the written permission of the publisher.

For information write:

Maznaim Publishing Corporation
4304 12th Avenue
Brooklyn, New York 11219

Printed in the United States of America

Printed by
MORIAH OFFSET CO.
115 Empire Boulevard
Brooklyn, N.Y. 11225
718—693-3800

EDITOR'S PREFACE

The Hebrew original of *Meam Lo'ez* on Ruth is a rich anthology of commentaries and individual insights culled from traditional sources. Rabbi Shmuel Yerushalmi aimed for completeness, and each entry is documented by reference to source and/or author. The serious student and scholar will benefit greatly by consulting these references.

This translation includes all of the original material, adapted and rearranged to weave the commentaries and individual insights into a narrative that would read like an enlarged "book of Ruth." The many voices of our sages have for over two thousand years elaborated on the implications of the text of the scripture, and the present volume is an integration of these elaborations. Out of the multicity, and seeming disparity of these voices, a unity of development has been achieved that illumines the interplay of themes and the complexity of detail subsumed in the book of Ruth itself. Apart from elaborations of the original story line, the reader can see how Torah law (halacha) structured many aspects of life for the Jew in Biblical times.

In keeping with our purpose, all references have been deleted and the interested reader can locate them in the Hebrew original by matching corresponding texts.

It has been a great pleasure to collaborate with E. van Handel both in the translation and initial editing of this work.

INTRODUCTION

Abba Zaira said: The book of Ruth contains neither laws of purity and impurity, nor precepts of forbidden and permitted. Then why was it written? Because of loving-kindness; to teach how greatly God rewards those who do kindness (Ruth Rabbah 2).

The Megillah of Ruth ends by recording the lineage of King David, founder of the dynasty of Judean kings, ancestor of the long-awaited Messiah, and a father of his people. For David, king of Israel, ranks with the patriarchs; just as God is called "the God of Abraham, the God of Isaac, and the God of Jacob" (Exodus 3:6), so is He called "the God of David" (2 Kings 20:5).

Yet this father of his people was subject to scathing abuse because of his descent from Ruth the Moabite. The Torah prohibits Moabite converts from marrying into God's congregation; as the scripture writes, "A Moabite shall not enter into the assembly of the Lord" (Deuteronomy 23:4). Ruth, however, was permitted to do so, on the basis of a long-forgotten law (halacha) that the prohibition applies only to the men of Moab, not to the women: "a Moabite, not a Moabitess." Yet in the time of King Saul, Doeg the Edomite, head of the Sanhedrin, tried to disqualify David from the kingship by proclaiming him unfit to enter God's congregation (Talmud).

Doeg's challenge touched off a heated controversy. The Talmud records that Amasa, son of Yitra, drew his sword and declared, "He who does not accept this halacha will be pierced by the sword. This is the tradition I received from the court of Samuel: A Moabite [is forbidden], not a Moabitess" (Yebamoth 77a).

A query was then dispatched to the aged prophet Samuel, who confirmed Amasa's statement: that aspect of the law was an oral tradition faithfully transmitted from Moses. Thereupon the prophet composed the Megillah of Ruth as a halachic ruling to validate David's right to enter the congregation.

According to a different opinion, when Samuel saw David seated on the throne, he wrote the Megillah in order to publicize the wonders of God in creating the possibility of the salvation of mankind—"the light of the Messiah," of whom all the prophets prophesied and whose coming is

Introduction

a basic tenet of Judaism. It reveals that the Messiah will be of the royal family of Judah, and therefore worthy of judging the poor and oppressing their oppressors, ruling the nations and bringing them all to a recognition of God.

After narrating how Ruth joined the people of Israel, wed Boaz, and bore Obed, "the father of Ishai, father of David" (v. 4:17), Samuel wrote: "And these are the generations of Peretz" (v. 4:18). Thus he exalted David by tracing his lineage back to Judah's son Peretz (lit. "the breaker"), the father of kings who break through to make way for themselves. And David was to say, "Behold, I have come to honor and greatness; in the scroll (*megillah*, מגילה) of a book it is written of me" (Psalms 40:8).

The Story and its Purposes

Samuel begins the account with the departure of the aristocratic Elimelech of Judah, his wife Naomi, and their sons from the famine-stricken land of Israel. After settling in Moab, Elimelech dies, followed by the death of both sons, who had married the Gentile women Orpah and Ruth. Naomi, destitute and bitter, sets out for the land of Israel, and she is joined by her daughters-in-law. When she pleads with them to turn back, Orpah leaves; Ruth, however, cleaves to Naomi and her God, and the two make their way together to the Holy Land. There Ruth goes to glean in the field of Naomi's kin, Boaz, who treats her kindly; and when the harvest season ends, Naomi sends her to ask him, as a redeemer, to marry her. Boaz at first offers a closer relative the opportunity of redeeming Ruth, and when the other refuses, marries her himself and begets Obed, grandfather of David.

According to our sages, the book has another purpose besides that of recording David's ancestry. It recounts the story of Ruth in lengthy detail, to teach us how magnificently God rewards those who practice kindness.

Thus Naomi says to Orpah and Ruth: "May the Lord deal kindly with you as you have dealt with the deceased and with me" (v. 1:8), from which our sages infer that they provided shrouds for their deceased husbands, relinquished their marriage settlements (*kethuboth*, כתובות) in favor of Naomi, and then supported her and shared in her misery. God would reward them for these acts of kindness. Because Orpah had accompanied Naomi forty paces, her descendant Goliath would be spared for forty days. Ruth, who accompanied her all the way back to the land of Israel and converted, merited that David and Solomon would descend from her. And Boaz merited the same by his kindness to Ruth.

This is the basis of faith in God. Although the reward is sometimes delayed, the Divine Master can be depended upon to reward in full measure.

The Megillah also emphasizes the long-range impact of one's deeds. Elimelech, though descended from the eminent Nachshon, son of Aminadav, begot sons who married Moabite women and died childless at an early age; Ruth, the sincere convert, had descendants who sat on the throne of Israel.

From the book of Ruth we learn, moreover, that God watches over men and requites each according to his deeds. Thus Eglon king of Moab, because he honored God (Judges 3:18), merited to have Ruth and David descend from him; but Elimelech, who left the Holy Land to avoid dispensing his money to the hungry populace, lost all and left his wife destitute. Then Ruth and Naomi chose poverty in the land of Israel over wealth at the royal palace of Moab, and they were raised to kingship.

Furthermore, the Megillah teaches that God arranges circumstances to implement His designs, without interfering with man's exercise of free will. Elimelech left the land of Israel and his sons married Moabites— while God thereby arranged for the seed of David to be brought back from Moab by Ruth. Similarly, God had arranged for Judah's tryst with Tamar to produce Peretz. Earlier still, Jacob had journeyed to Laban, who tried to thwart him in every way and tricked him into wedding Leah in addition to Rachel, even as God had ordained them to be the mothers of the twelve tribes.

Because these three episodes are part of the same plan, they are all mentioned in the blessing which the elders bestowed upon Boaz and Ruth at the time of their marriage: "May the Lord make the woman who is coming into your house of Israel like Rachel and like Leah. . . . And may your house be like the house of Peretz whom Tamar bore to Judah, from the seed that the Lord will give you from this young woman" (v. 4:11,12).

In the order of the Holy Scripture, the book of Ruth is followed by Psalms, to teach that Ruth's suffering had a worthwhile end. From her came David who overflowed before God with songs and praise.

Although the book of Ruth was written by the prophet Samuel, it is included among the Writings rather than the Prophets. Apparently it stemmed from a lower level of prophecy than the book of Judges and the book of Samuel composed by the same prophet.

Why Ruth is Read on Shavuoth (Pentecost)

The Megillah of Ruth is read in the synagogue on the festival of Shavuoth, "the time of the giving of our Torah."

What connection is there between Ruth and *Matan Torah* (מתן תורה, the giving of the Law)? One answer is that the account of Ruth's marriage to Boaz testifies to the authenticity of the Oral Law rendered to Moses at Sinai. The legitimacy of David and of the Messiah depends on the halachic distinction "a Moabite, not a Moabitess," which is an oral tradition not recorded in the scripture.

Our sages declare that the book of Ruth is read on Shavuoth to teach that the Torah is given only through affliction and poverty. "The Torah said before God: If the rich study me, they will grow haughty. But when the poor study me, they know they are hungry and lowly, and will not grow haughty."

Ruth personifies the teaching that the Torah is perpetuated only by those who make do with little, suffer, and accept death for its sake. She joined the Jewish people and made do with barley, the bread of poverty; endured wandering, want, and loneliness; and she cleaved to the Torah even if she would have to die for it, declaring, "Where you die, I will die" (v. 1:17). Therefore, she merited to have Solomon as her descendant, who made the Torah accessible to others through his wisdom.

This, too, we learn from Ruth: One should not study Torah in order to achieve honor and glory, although these will come. She cleaved to the bitter, destitute Naomi, and in the end attained honor and glory in this world and in the next. Thus Boaz said to her, "The Lord repay your deed [in this world], and be your reward complete [in the World to Come]" (v. 2:12).

From Elimelech, on the other hand, we learn that one should not leave the land of Israel. Yet one may do so in order to study Torah (Talmud).

"How great is the illumination provided by the Torah!" exclaim our sages. Gentiles abandon their vanities and convert in order to cleave to it; how much more so, then, must we exalt it and toil to possess it!

Just as our forefathers accepted the Torah and entered a covenant with God through ritual immersion, so, too, did Ruth at her conversion. From the time she joined Israel "at the beginning of the barley harvest" (v. 1:22) (on Passover, where the first-grain (the *omer*, עֹמֶר) of barley is offered) until the end of the barley harvest on Shavuoth, she was purified and elevated by suffering, just as the children of Israel were purified and elevated during seven weeks from the Exodus on Passover until *Matan Torah* on Shavuoth.

We learn as well not to look down on the proselyte. Rabbi Akiba was descended from converts, and according to the Midrash was worthy of having the Torah given through him, had he not been preceded by Moses. Thus the Midrash recounts that when Moses ascended on high and saw Rabbi Akiba, he said to God, "You have such a one, yet You give the Torah through me!"

Ruth's great-grandson David is likened to Moses. Whatever Moses did, says the Midrash, David did also. Moses saved Israel from the Egyptian bondage, David, from suppression by the nations. Moses split the sea, David, the rivers. Moses gave Israel the Five Books of the Torah, David, the five books of Psalms.

Ruth was forty years old when she embraced the Torah, and perhaps it was her example that inspired Rabbi Akiba to begin learning Torah at the same age. Hence adults who received no Torah education in childhood can draw courage to educate and immerse themselves in Torah.

From Ruth's divinely chosen husband—the wealthy aristocratic Boaz, of whom it is written, "Boaz ate and drank, and his heart was glad [with Torah study]" (v. 3:7), we learn that the rich, too, must occupy themselves with Torah learning.

The story of Boaz and Ruth teaches that righteous women are equal to righteous men. Although women are not obligated to engage in Torah study, they can attain high spiritual levels, as did the beautiful Ruth, who, by carefully observing the laws of *leket* (gleaning) and scrupulously practicing modesty, merited to become the mother of royalty.

The book of Ruth is read during the harvest season to remind us that Torah study is a prerequisite for prosperity. When "It came to pass in the days of the judging of the judges," which our sages explain as reflecting a weakening of Torah study, "there was a famine in the land" (v. 1:1).

It also reminds us of the obligation of giving to the poor from the harvest, in accordance with the laws of *peah*, *leket*, and *shikechah* (Leviticus 19:9–10). Charity is particularly necessary and advisable at the completion of the days of Counting the Omer, a time of *din* (דין), strict judgment, for it then protects the giver from the Attribute of Justice (*Din*).

Through charity and Torah study, Israel will merit the speedy coming of Ruth's descendant, the Messiah.

THE BOOK OF RUTH

MeAm Lo'ez

RUTH 1

1:1 וַיְהִי בִּימֵי שְׁפֹט הַשֹּׁפְטִים וַיְהִי רָעָב בָּאָרֶץ וַיֵּלֶךְ אִישׁ מִבֵּית לֶחֶם יְהוּדָה לָגוּר בִּשְׂדֵי מוֹאָב הוּא וְאִשְׁתּוֹ וּשְׁנֵי בָנָיו:

It came to pass in the days of the judging of the judges, that there was a famine in the land. There went a man from Bethlehem in Judah to dwell in the Fields of Moab—he, his wife, and his two sons.

This book of the Holy Scripture unfolds the divine pattern of events that was to give rise to the royal house of David as a result of the marriage of Boaz and the Moabite woman Ruth. It is the story of how Ruth earned the privilege of becoming the mother of royalty in Israel because of her persistence in cleaving to the Jewish people.

The narrative begins by recording that these events took place in the days of the judges. The age of the kings was still in the future, and the leadership of the people was in the hands of chieftain-judges. It was the time of Ibetzan, that is, Boaz.

But they were not simply the days of the judges; they were the days of "the judging of the judges." They were the days, our sages point out, when the judges were being judged.

If a judge would point out a small offense committed by a Jew, the Jew would point out a worse offense committed by the judge. If the judge rebuked someone for an obvious wrongdoing, the man would reply that the misdeeds of the judge were equally grave, although harder to detect. And if he was chastised for sinning in private, he would retort that the judge had sinned in public.

The inference by our sages that the judges were judged, is hinted at in the words שְׁפֹט הַשֹּׁפְטִים, whose letters can be arranged to read שָׁפְטוּ שׁוֹפְטֵיהֶם—"they judged their judges."

In judging their judges, the people did not stop at mere words. Before a judge could order an offender flogged, the offender would flog the judge.

Besides judging the judges and rejecting their rebuke, the people also found fault with the judiciary process itself. For the judges were struck

[3]

by fear of violent defendants and failed to convict them. They were thus guilty of transgressing the admonition לא תגורו מפני איש, "be not intimidated by any man" (Deut. 1:17), and the growing epidemic of crime that swept the land went unchecked.

Thus King Solomon was to declare: "These also are [sayings] from the wise: To show respect for persons in judgment is not good. If one says to the wicked: 'You are righteous,' people will curse him, nations shall fume at him" (Proverbs 24:23, 24).

Those who pervert justice are cursed for the consequences that ensue.

Accordingly, the book of Ruth opens on a note of distress. The expression *vayehi* (וַיְהִי), "and it came to pass," contains the word *vay* (וַי), "woe." Woe to the Jews in those times!

Woe to a generation that judges its judges. And woe to a generation whose judges deserve to be judged!

The Consequences

Because it was a generation that judged its judges, there were no men of sufficient merit among them to intercede before God and forestall the decree of famine that was brought on by the corruption of society.

Just as Israel fell short of being a perfectly righteous nation, their judges fell short of being ideal rulers. Ideally, a ruler in Israel guides the people by his personal example and his strong, inspired leadership. But the judges did not provide effective leadership, and the people did not attain spiritual perfection.

The ideal society cannot exist without justice in law. Thus, when Jacob prophesied about the Messianic age, he said: "The staff will not depart from Judah, nor the law-giver from between his feet, until Shilo (the Messiah) will come . . ." (Genesis 49:10). The Messianic king will rebuke all who are within his hearing; he will smite them with the rod of his mouth (cf. Isaiah 11:3,4).

The people had the leaders they deserved, and the corruption of both deepened. As a result, the society crumbled. There came true the words of Isaiah: "They that lead the people cause them to err; and they that are led by them are destroyed" (Isaiah 9:15).

Then God brought judgment upon Israel in the form of a famine.

Famine is a harsh punishment. But this famine was at the same time an act of divine providence. It would provide Israel with a righteous king, David, king of Israel, who would administer universal justice.

Accordingly, God patterned events and arranged causes that led to Elimelech's leaving the country, and Naomi's bringing back Ruth the Moabite.

Troubled Times

The period of the judges, before the monarchy was established, was a difficult period for the Jewish people.

With no king to unite the twelve tribes and lead a strong army into battle, they were continually harrassed by the neighboring nations and subjugated.

Their physical woes reflected their spiritual decline. When Israel cleaves to the Torah, God casts fear of them upon the nations. But without the forceful guidance of a king, they failed to attain the required level of cleaving to the Torah that God demands of them, and He delivered Israel into the hands of its enemies.

In the days when the events recorded in the book of Ruth took place, famine was added to Israel's woes. The famine was all the more devastating because there was no king to stabilize food prices, distribute available food fairly, or compel the rich to support the poor. Since the judges had no power over the people, food was hoarded and prices soared.

Then, to add to their woes, Elimelech abandoned them. A great man of noble lineage and vast wealth, to whom the starving populace looked for support and encouragement during the famine, had crushed their morale by leaving. And there was no king to prevent his departure.

These three calamities are alluded to in the three *vay's* ("woes") of the verse: *vay'ehi*, in the days of the judging of the judges; *vay'ehi*, there was a famine; *vay'elech*, and Elimelech left.

More on "The Judging of the Judges"

The scripture records about those times that "also to their judges they did not listen" (Judges 2:17). And because the people judged their judges, in punishment, measure for measure, Israel was judged by one of God's four "judgments" spoken of by the prophet Ezekiel: "For thus said the Lord God: How much more so when I send My four sore judgments against Jerusalem, the sword, and the famine, and the evil beasts, and the pestilence, to cut off from it man and beast" (Ezekiel 14:21).

Famine is the judgment that comes upon the world when justice is delayed (*inuy ha'din*, עִנּוּי הַדִּין) or perverted (*ivuth ha'din*, עִוּוּת הַדִּין).

In this sense too, then, "it was in the days of the judging of the judges"; that is, the judges of the heavenly tribunal judged the judges of the generation. Their decree: there was to be a famine in the land.

The famine for bread was the physical manifestation of a famine for spiritual sustenance. The word of God, Torah, is also called bread (Proverbs 9:5), and because the people of Israel had neglected to nourish their souls by the study of Torah, neither were their bodies nourished.

This accords with the words of the Talmud that "If there is no Torah, there is no flour" (Avoth). There was both a hunger for bread and a hunger for Torah when Elimelech abandoned the land of Israel for the land of Moab.

Famine also comes upon the world on account of strife. Compromise and peace are necessary for abundance, as it is written, "He puts peace as your border, and satiates you with the fat of wheat" (Psalms 147:14). Without peace, there is no abundance.

Israel in those days was not a harmonious whole but a people divided and quarreling among themselves. As a result, "it was in the days of the judging of the judges." Since no side would yield in any dispute, the judges were kept busy judging the claims and complaints of the people.

Symptomatic of the disunity is the fact that Israel was governed by "judges" (plural), rather than by a single judge. Because Torah knowledge had declined and qualified leaders were scarce, all who wished declared themselves judges.

Our Sages derive from the combination of singular (שפט) and plural (שופטים) forms in the verse that two judges would govern at the same time. In contrast to the self-declared judges, these are identified as being qualified judges.

Barak and Deborah were two of those judges. Between them they led the people to victory on the battlefield, and together then offered praise to God (Judges 5).

According to the Midrash, there were then actually three righteous judges. The third was Yael, wife of Chever the Kenite, who contributed to victory by slaying the enemy general Sisera (Judges 4:21).

That she, too, was a judge is apparent from the Song of Deborah:

"In the days of Shamgar the son of Anath, in the days of Yael, the highways ceased and the travellers walked through byways" (Judges 5:6). [On account of her forceful administration of justice, the roads were safe.]

Rabbi Yehoshua ben Levi identifies the judges as Ehud and Shamgar, the latter having begun to rule before the former died. Thus it is written: "And after [Ehud] was Shamgar son of Anath . . . and Ehud died" (Judges 3:31, 4:1).

The Book of Judges records of their time that "The children of Israel continued to do evil in the eyes of God" (Judges 4:1). The people sinned, and the result was the famine.

Ehud lived in the beginning of the era of the judges, shortly after the land of Israel had been conquered and apportioned to the tribes. In their eagerness to work the new fields and vineyards God had given them, the Israelites neglected Torah study, whereupon God delivered them into the hands of Eglon, king of Moab (Judges 3:12).

According to the view, therefore, that the story of Ruth took place in the time of Ehud, Elimelech left for a country and a nation that was then oppressing the people of Israel, even as he himself was guilty of oppressing them by failing to provide for the poor, and crushing their spirit by his departure.

Then "Ehud made a sword that had two mouths" (Judges 3:16). Our sages explain that he upheld the study of Torah, which is called a double-mouthed sword, for it nourishes a man in this world and in the World to Come.

Elaborating on the verse "The voice is the voice of Jacob, and the hands are the hands of Esau" (Genesis 27:22), the Talmud declares that when the voice of Jacob is raised in Torah study, the arm of Esau can no longer prevail in battle. Ehud slew Eglon by the sword and freed Israel from the yoke of Moab, and then, by having restored the study of Torah among the people, helped Israel keep free of Moab.

It is thus clear that the criticism leveled by our sages was only at the majority of the people. Righteous individuals were still to be found, such as Deborah and Barak, Shamgar and Ehud—and Ibetzan (Boaz).

Another interpretation: "It was in the days of the judging of the judges"—it was a time when God applied the attribute of stern justice (*Din*) to the judges themselves. When God brings judgment upon the world, He begins with the judges, because they cause anguish to the poor.

Thus the scripture writes, "Wherever [the judges] went forth, the hand of the Lord was against them for evil . . . and they were sore distressed" (Judges 2:15). He caused the judges to suffer, and in addition brought famine to the land.

Others perceive yet another reason for the scripture linking famine and "the judging of the judges." It is based on the teaching of our sages that Jerusalem was destroyed because "they set their words upon the words of the Torah." That is, the judges of the time did not seek to make peace among the litigants, but applied the strict letter of the law. "Let the law pierce the mountain!" was their credo—and famine and destruction followed.

The generation was not punished by exile, however, because it cherished the land. This is demonstrated by the fact that the scripture highlights the single instance of this one man, Elimelech, who left the land to escape the famine.

Some say that Elimelech left for fear of the disunity and strife that increased in the wake of the famine. The stress of general want aggravated tensions, and seeing how troublesome it would be for him as a judge to deal with the many disputes that would come before him, he fled.

Other men of stature also refused to undertake the troublesome burden of serving as judges, with the result, as already noted, that unworthy judges were appointed, whom the people then had good cause to condemn.

In Praise of Israel

In this view, the people themselves were mostly praiseworthy, and the book of Ruth itself attests to their careful observation of Torah Law. They gave the "gifts of the poor" (Leviticus 19:9,10): they left the corner (*peah*, פאה) of the fields untouched, for the poor to reap; and let them pick (*leket*, לקט) stalks of grain that dropped during reaping; and gather forgotten sheaves of cut grain (*shikechah*, שכחה). They performed conversions according to Torah law, as in the case of Ruth herself; refrained from marrying Moabite women converts, although permitted by law since the halacha had not been clarified at that time; arranged for fields to be redeemed by relatives, as Boaz did; married in the presence of ten male Jews (v. 4:2); and acquired ownership of property by passing a kerchief (v. 4:7)—*kinyan sudar*, קנין סודר—as provided for in Torah law.

They were chaste. Ruth spent days picking in the fields, but the fieldhands never touched her. Boaz awoke one night to find a beautiful woman at his feet, but he did not sin.

They had faith in God. Boaz greeted the harvesters with "the Lord be with you," and they replied, "May the Lord bless you" (v. 2:4).

Our sages comment upon the verse, "God spoke to Moses and Aaron and gave them instructions regarding the children of Israel . . ." (Exodus 6:13): God said to them, "My children are dissenters, are excitable, are troublesome." Rabbi Avigdor Miller explains this in a positive manner: They are aggressive and take action; and if they see their leaders in the wrong, they oppose them, as they did here in "judging the judges."

This is usually held against them: Woe to the generation which judges its judges! But this can also be seen as a commendation of our fathers. They criticized their leaders; and therefore the leaders were forced to be perfect, else they would be exposed to public censure.

On the one hand, the children of Israel were "troublesome," they were aggressive, and they attacked the leaders for every deviation, real or imagined. We stand horrified when Moses exclaimed: "A little more, and they will stone me" (Exodus 17:4), and we might consider them an unruly rabble. But these words ought to be put on a banner and displayed as a testament to the greatness of our forefathers. Even Moses could not escape their censure. Authority meant nothing to them when they thought they saw corruption.

"My children are troublesome" is thus the explanation of why they are "My children." Their loyalty to God transcends their loyalty to men.

The Mistress is Stricken

According to this view that the people were righteous, it was thus the failure and incompetence of the judges that brought on the famine. "Justice, justice shall you seek," exhorts the Torah (Deuteronomy 16:20), "so that you will live and inherit the land!" And our sages conclude that the appointment of worthy judges sustains the people of Israel and keeps them on their land.

Conversely, the lack of justice must lead to a lack of food. And since this was a time when the judges deserved to be judged, the land was stricken with famine.

As the pillar of justice eroded, the channels of rainfall broke down. Ordinarily, the whole world is blessed with rain in the merit of the land of Israel, as it is written: "Who gives rain on the face of the land [of Israel] and [then] sends water on the face of lands outside [*chutzoth*, חוצות]" (Job 5:10). But now the land of Israel was afflicted with famine, while in the other lands (including Moab, according to one view) there was no famine. The mistress was stricken, the maidservant was not stricken.

Hence *vay'ehi* ("woe")—how great the tragedy that God had to bring famine because of the sins of His creatures!

The stark contrast between Moab's plenty and Israel's want should have alerted the judges to examine their deeds and repent, for the famine in Israel was obviously not a natural phenomenon, but a divine punishment.

Elimelech did not do so, and instead of repenting, fled.

By fleeing, he demonstrated his lack of faith in God. In contrast stands the episode of the gentile who pointed out to a Torah scholar who was leaving the land of Israel to seek his livelihood elsewhere: "God Who provides for you outside the Holy Land will provide for you in it as well." [And he shamed him into staying (Talmud).]

Others also blame the famine on the people, who were ambivalent in their faith. Some served idols, others served God, and they thought themselves clever. "If we are right," the first reasoned, "the idols will bless us. If we are wrong, the merits of our God-fearing neighbors will shield us from God's wrath." But God brought famine upon them all.

Elimelech's Flight

"How greatly God cherishes the ascent to the land of Israel!" exclaim our sages. In describing the return to Zion in the days of Ezra, the scripture gives a detailed account of the returning population, down to its horses, camels, and mules (Ezra 2). But when the wealthy Elimelech left the land, the scripture merely says: "a man went."

Both in this and the following verse, the scripture says that Elimelech was "a man . . . from Bethlehem in Judah." Although he was "a man" (*ish*, איש), a person of rank, wealth, and distinction, and hence under obligation to protect the poor, he abandoned them and left the country. Although "from Bethlehem in Judah," one of its old and established citizens, he went with his family to settle permanently in Moab. Thus the following verse says, significantly, "They came to the Fields of Moab and *they were there.*" What is emphasized is that they had left not merely as a temporary measure but to remain there.

Not only did he leave the Holy Land for the unholy soil and the land of the gentiles, he left Bethlehem, the home of Boaz and later of the righteous Ishai and his son David. None of this he considered or anticipated.

One of the reasons he fled was that the people were judging their judges. "If this is so in times of prosperity," he thought, "how much worse it will be in times of stress and famine. The land will be ridden with crime, and there is no one to restrain the criminal!" [Evidently he left before the famine deepened.]

Elimelech was "a man," a prominent member of the family of Nachshon son of Aminadav, prince of the tribe of Judah during the exodus from Egypt. And he is identified in the next verse as Elimelech (*elimelech*, אֱלִימֶלֶךְ), which literally means "a king to me" (*elai melech*, אֵלַי מֶלֶךְ). He saw himself as the progenitor of kings, and, being of the tribe of Judah, even sought the royal scepter for himself. For, as he was wont to exclaim, "(אֵלַי מֶלֶךְ) Kingship will come to me!" (Talmud.)

He failed to understand, however, that the essence of kingship is charity and kindness: the king's task is to care for the needs of the people. When the time came to appoint a king over Israel, God chose a shepherd who faithfully and tenderly cared for the flocks entrusted to him. "He chose David, His servant, and took him from the sheepfolds. From following the ewes that give suck He brought him to shepherd Jacob, His people, and Israel, His inheritance. He shepherded them according to the integrity of his heart, and by the skillfulness of his hands he led them" (Psalms 78:70–72).

Thus when David's son Solomon was asked about the power of charity, he replied: Look at what my father said: "He has distributed and given to the needy, his righteousness (*tzedaka*, צדקה—lit. charity) endures forever, his horn shall be exalted in honor" (Psalms 112:9).

Elimelech closed his hand to the needy, and thus disqualified himself for kingship. He failed to realize that the honors of royalty go to the one who seeks the public welfare, not personal glory.

On the other hand, he sought the kingship also because the people were judging their judges, making it impossible to enforce any verdict and to punish criminals. The same motivation, later, was behind the people's request for a king when they said to the prophet Samuel: "Give us a king to judge us" (1 Samuel 8:5). They wanted justice enforced against powerful men who defied the law.

In Elimelech's day, however, the time was not yet ripe for the monarchy. This had to await the unfolding of events that stemmed from the portentous encounter between Jacob and Esau, as recounted in the Portion of VaYishlach (Genesis 32,33).

At that encounter Jacob had said to Esau, "Let my master pass before his servant" (Genesis 33:14). For this to come true, says the Talmud, eight kings had to first rule in Edom, the inheritance of Esau, before any king reigned in Israel. Since the reigns of the eight Edomite kings were not yet completed in Elimelech's time, Israel had to still remain under the rule of the judges.

At that historic meeting, too, according to our sages, all the members of Jacob's household—except for Rachel, who was shielded by Joseph, and her son Benjamin, who had not yet been born—had bowed down before Esau. Therefore only a descendant of Rachel would be able to vanquish Israel's arch-enemy Amalek, descended from Esau.

Since the task of Israel's first king would be to destroy Amalek, he would thus have to be of the tribe of Benjamin, not of Judah. That king was Saul.

For all these reasons Elimelech was not appointed king. Neither was he appointed chieftain-judge, for that function was already served by Boaz.

Others explain Elimelech's claim to kingship thus. [It was not simply the expression of personal ambition, or a means of dealing with the immediate problems of his society, but] the prophetic vision of a *Gadol HaDor*, the great man of his generation, who saw in the future a magnificent chain of kings arising from him, extending through David, Hezekiah (Chizkiya), and the Messiah. On the other hand he saw the corruption of his generation due to the failure of the judges, and the resulting famine. So he tried to hasten the establishment of the monarchy by going to Moab in search of the "precious pearl" that would lead, he knew, to the founding of Israel's royal dynasty.

Amidst the licentious populace of the Fields of Moab he thought to find one chaste and modest woman—outstanding on that account—who would be worthy of becoming the mother of royalty in Israel.

[His vision came true, in fact, although indirectly, by Boaz eventually taking Ruth in levirate marriage, whose purpose, according to the

Law of Moses, is "to establish the name of his brother in Israel" (Deuteronomy 25:7). The resulting progeny was thus a continuation of the house of Elimelech.]

It is revealing in this regard that וַיֵּלֶךְ ("went") appears twice in the Holy Scripture—the "going" of Elimelech and the "going" (וַיֵּלֶךְ) of Amram, the father of Moses. Of Amram it is written: "A man of the house of Levi went and took to wife the daughter of Levi" (Exodus 2:1). Of Elimelech it is written: "A man went from Bethlehem in Judah." Just as Amram's going illuminated the world with Moses, who redeemed Israel from Egypt, so did Elimelech's going sow the seeds of the Messiah, who will redeem Israel from the nations.

Elimelech was not the only distinguished member of his family. His wife was Naomi (*naomi*, נעמי—"the pleasant") known far and wide for her good deeds that were pleasing to God and to man. And their sons were "Ephratites"—people of distinction. So well known were they that here the scripture does not find it necessary to identify them by recording their lineage.

"There went a man . . . he, his wife, and his . . . sons." First the man went alone, to ascertain that there was food in Moab, and also where in the Fields of Moab to settle. Then he returned to take his family, and he, his wife, and his sons went away together.

Naomi had no desire to leave the Holy Land, but thought it proper to follow her husband; and the sons followed their parents. Thus our sages declare: "He, his wife, and his sons—they are listed in order of importance. Since Elimelech led the departure, he was punished first."

Although he only had his wife and two sons to provide for, he fled to the land of the Moabites, about whom the scripture says: "You shall not seek their peace nor their prosperity all your days forever" (Deuteronomy 23:7).

He was the scion of a noble family, bearing the seed of kings. Yet he forsook the Holy Land and abandoned the people to their misery.

When Elimelech left the land, say our sages, God was sitting in judgment of the world, His heavenly tribunal in session before Him. At first God concealed Elimelech; thus the scripture records that "there went a man" without mentioning his name. But the Attribute of Justice mentioned his name—as the next verse records: "And the name of the man was Elimelech"—and immediately a harsh decree was issued against him and his sons.

It was not hunger that drove him to leave. There was food aplenty in his house: he went from "Bethlehem," literally, "a house of bread." He left for fear that the poor would beg him for food.

Significant, then, is the emphasis that he left for Moab as "a man" (*ish*, איש), a person of stature and wealth, and there he became impoverished as a punishment for abandoning the poor.

The punishment befit the deed also in that, of all places, he chose to live in Moab. Although the Moabites were descended from Abraham's nephew Lot, they had not come out to welcome the Israelites in the wilderness with bread and water. Therefore, God had commanded Israel "Do not seek their peace or their prosperity" (Deuteronomy, 23:7), and He had forbidden the Jewish people to marry male Moabite converts.

Like Moab, Elimelech did not offer Israel food and water. He forsook the people in violation of the command to "Love your neighbor as yourself" (Leviticus 19:18) and he went to live among a people whose prosperity a Jew is forbidden to seek.

By departing for Moab, Elimelech thus brought darkness upon Israel by helping in their subjugation. Yet out of his going there gleamed forth the light of the Messiah of the house of David.

Elimelech's departure, though criticized, is not unprecedented. His forebear Judah, whose name appears in this verse, also left his brethren at one point to live among gentiles, as it is written: "It came to pass at that time, that Judah went down from his brothers, and turned to a certain Adullamite, whose name was Hirah" (Genesis 38:1). And the events that followed led to the completion of an early chapter in the history of the monarchy. [Judah's ringing confession, "She is more righteous than I" (Genesis 38:26), won him the kingship forever, and the child Peretz born to Judah and the convert Tamar was a link in the chain leading to David and the Messiah.]

Furthermore, the next verse points out that Elimelech and his family remained righteous in Moab as they had been in the land of Israel. The mane was still Elimelech, worthy of kingship; the wife was still Naomi, whose deeds are pleasing; and the two sons remained Ephratites, men of distinction.

Had Elimelech's purpose in leaving been simply to obtain food, he could have remained in the land of Israel but moved near the border, where he could purchase food from Moab. But his purpose was "to sojourn" in Moab.

Another interpretation is that originally he intended only to live in Moab temporarily ("to sojourn"). But in the end, he settled there permanently.

In contrast to Boaz (Ibetzan), who was burdened with the support of thirty sons and thirty daughters (Judges 12:9), yet did not leave the Holy Land during the famine, Elimelech left although he had only two sons to support. Therefore Boaz merited the kingship that Elimelech sought.

Another criticism leveled against Elimelech is that he did not leave the land of Israel during the entire time injustice was rampant there: He left only when the famine came and the lack of justice affected him personally. This is reflected in the sequence of the verse. He did not leave "in the days of the judging of the judges," i.e., when the judges were being judged; but after "there was a famine in the land." Only then "there went a man from Bethlehem in Judah."

Similarly, in the infamous *Pilegesh beGivah* episode (Judges 19,20), the Benjaminites were slaughtered because they protested for the honor of mortals but not against the idol of Mica (Judges 17).

One might try to defend Elimelech by citing the dictum of our sages: "In time of famine, leave your home." However, that does not mean one is allowed to leave the Holy Land. Furthermore, it does not apply to great men, who must not abandon their people in order to seek their own welfare. A man of wealth should distribute his money among the poor; a sage should remain with his people to lend them moral support and pray that God grant them bread. Elimelech did not do so.

Elimelech did the opposite of what Abraham had done, who also left the land of Israel during a famine (Genesis 12:10). Abraham devoted his life to doing *chesed*, kindness. He lavished hospitality on wayfarers, and when he ran out of food to give, he went to Egypt, there to continue his kind practices. But Elimelech, who had food in the land of Israel, left in order to avoid doing *chesed* with it.

Abraham left the land when it was inhabited by wicked heathens; Elimelech left when it was settled by the Jewish people. Moreover, he left Bethlehem, the seat of the Sanhedrin, a city from which Torah came forth. For as King David later said: "Who will give me water [a metaphor for Torah] to drink from the cistern of Bethlehem at the gate [where the High Court of Sanhedrin convened]!" (2 Samuel 23:15.)

When a rich man sets out on a journey, the local poor see him off and he throws money into the crowd. Elimelech, however, was afraid of just

Ruth 1

that, and he left in secrecy. Hence the verse does not mention his name, saying only "there went a man."

On the other hand, upon arriving in Moab, he publicized his name—"the name of the man was Elimelech" (v. 1:2)—so that people would honor him.

Although a great man left, the people of Israel did not follow his example. Despite the famine, they remained in the Holy Land.

1:2 וְשֵׁם הָאִישׁ אֱלִימֶלֶךְ וְשֵׁם אִשְׁתּוֹ נָעֳמִי וְשֵׁם שְׁנֵי־בָנָיו מַחְלוֹן וְכִלְיוֹן אֶפְרָתִים מִבֵּית לֶחֶם יְהוּדָה וַיָּבֹאוּ שְׂדֵי־מוֹאָב וַיִּהְיוּ־שָׁם:

Now the name of the man was Elimelech, and the name of his wife, Naomi; and the name of his two sons, Machlon and Kilyon—Ephratites from Bethlehem [in] Judah. They came to the Fields of Moab, and they were there.

The man, his wife, and his two sons are now identified as Elimelech, Naomi, and Machlon and Kilyon. We are told that they were Ephratites, that is, distinguished people from the Judean town of Bethlehem.

Some Jews, when they find themselves in exile among gentiles, are ashamed of their Jewish names and change them. Not so Elimelech and his family. Even in Moab they kept their original names.

Everyone who saw these four foreigners recognized them immediately as distinguished Ephratites from Bethlehem.

The old saying, "in his hometown a man is known by his name, elsewhere he is known by his clothes," did not apply to them.

We learn from Naomi's name ("one who is pleasing") that she was a woman whose deeds were pleasing to God and man. However, she was punished because she had not prevented her husband from leaving the land of Israel, which was within her power. For by Torah law a man cannot force his wife to relocate, let alone leave the Holy Land.

The fate that befell this family in Moab is hinted at in the names of the two sons. In the scripture, Machlon and Kilyon are also called Yoash and Saraph (1 Chronicles 4:22), which means despair and burning. They despaired of God saving Israel from the famine, and by divine retribution, measure for measure, they deserved death by burning for leaving the Holy Land. For Torah Law forbids leaving the land of Israel except under certain conditions, and when one nullifies even a single aspect of Torah teaching, it is as if he burned the entire Torah.

It is significant that they were "two sons." They were of two minds and did not consult with one another. Another interpretation is that they were equal in greatness.

According to one view, Machlon and Kilyon were not their original names, but the names they were given to tell of their fate—dissolution and destruction. They were wiped off the face of the earth because they had left the Holy Land. Indeed, Machlon and Kilyon are not two distinct names, but a single name-form which reveals that they incurred extinction by the hand of God.

The name Machlon (מחלון) also conveys that they had made their lives *chullin* (חולין), commonplace and unworthy of preserving. Both were thus "Kilyon" (כליון)—subject to extinction (Kliyah, כליה).

On the other hand, the names are seen as distinguishing between them. Machlon also means forgiveness (*mechilah*, מחילה); he who married Ruth was forgiven for his sins. God left him a remembrance and perpetuated his name through his next-of-kin, Boaz. But Kilyon married Orpah, and as his name implies, was totally obliterated.

It is stressed that they were Ephratites; that is, they were distinguished because they came from Bethlehem in Judah. Although there were other towns in the land of Israel named Bethlehem, the most important town was that located in the territory of Judah, the tribe of royalty.

Our sages explain that "Ephratites" means nobles or princes. The fact that Eglon, king of Moab, gave his daughters Ruth and Orpah in marriage to Machlon and Kilyon, attests to their eminent stature.

Moreover, they were Ephratites because they traced their descent from the prophetess Miriam, who is called Ephrata (1 Chronicles 2:19). Yocheved and Miriam (Shifra and Puah of Exodus 1:15) had defied Pharaoh's orders to kill the newborns, and as their reward God promised them "houses" (Exodus 1:21)—a house of priesthood and a house of royalty.

Such was Miriam's faith in God, that even when her brother Moses was abandoned on the Nile, she did not despair. She had "stood from afar to see" (Exodus 2:4) how her prophecy would turn out in the end.

Accordingly, now that God's promise of a royal household was

Ruth 1

about to be fulfilled through this family, the scripture records that they were Ephratites, that is, descendants of Miriam.

Elimelech, Naomi, and their two sons had three virtues essential for kingship: wealth, wisdom, and eminent lineage. Elimelech was wealthy; Naomi, who attained prophecy, was wise; and Machlon and Kilyon were Ephratites. But all these virtues were of no avail when they left the land of Israel and the sons married Moabite women.

Originally they had gone to the "Fields of Moab," that is, they intended to live in one of the small ("field") towns. Finding that the townspeople were steeped in immorality, they moved to the larger cities. However, a water shortage in the cities forced their return to the towns, where they remained. It is stressed to their discredit that "they were there" despite the rampant depravity.

Another interpretation is that while at first Elimelech intended merely to sojourn in Moab for the duration of the famine, eventually the family settled there.

Accordingly, so long as Elimelech was only planning to live there temporarily, the scripture concealed his identity and merely stated that "a man went." But when he fixed his residence in Moab—"and they were there"—it proclaimed his infamy and recorded his name.

It is ironic that Elimelech chose Moab as a haven from hunger. The male converts of Moab were not even permitted to marry into the community of Israel, since, as already noted, they had not welcomed the Israelites in the desert with bread and water. Yet to this people, Elimelech now took his family in search of food.

By dwelling among the stingy, inhospitable Moabites, their own tendency to stinginess was reinforced. Thus the scripture records that they did not travel throughout the country, but stayed in one place. According to one interpretation, they hoped thereby to keep their arrival in Moab secret so that poor Jews would not come asking for food.

Another interpretation is that the scripture testifies to their merit; although "they were there"—in depraved, inhospitable Moab—they remained unaffected. In Moab they retained the same level of piety as in the Holy Land. Similarly, the scripture had written of Joseph: "And God was with Joseph . . . and he was in the house of his master the Egyptian" (Genesis 39:2). Although he was the only Jew in Egypt, he had remained faithful to God.

1:3 וַיָּמָת אֱלִימֶלֶךְ אִישׁ נָעֳמִי וַתִּשָּׁאֵר הִיא וּשְׁנֵי בָנֶיהָ:

Then Elimelech, Naomi's husband, died; and she was left with her two sons.

After leaving the land of Israel, Naomi was struck down by one tragedy after another. Following their arrival in Moab, her husband died, and she was left alone with her two sons.

Elimelech incurred the punishment of death on two accounts: for leaving the land of Israel, and for closing his hand to the poor.

As for Naomi, she was so well known that Elimelech is here identified as "Naomi's husband." Her personal prominence added to his prestige. Thus later, when she returned, the people simply said, "Is this Naomi?" instead of identifying her as Elimelech's wife.

Naomi epitomized the woman of valor praised by King Solomon: "Her husband is known in the gates when he sits among the elders of the land" (Proverbs 31:23). It is a measure of the righteous woman that all speak of the man as the husband of such a wife. Here, too, the scripture reveals that Elimelech was famous on account of Naomi's activities. And he is remembered because of her.

[Although at that time Jewish men were permitted to take more than one wife,] it is stressed that Elimelech had always been "Naomi's husband." He had refrained from taking another wife, lest her children dispossess Naomi's children of their inheritance.

Elimelech had remained faithful to his wife even amidst the immorality of Moab. Generations earlier, the Moabites had succeeded in corrupting some of the Israelites in the wilderness, including even Zimri, leader of the tribe of Simeon. Yet Elimelech did not succumb.

His staunch loyalty to Naomi would have had a powerful influence on his sons; had he lived, they would have shunned Moabite women. After his death, however, they married Moabite wives, and Naomi, now alone, was unable to stop them.

Elaborating on this verse, our sages comment: "Everyone is destined to die, everyone is headed for death. Happy is the man who departs the world with a good name." This did not come true for Elimelech. The scripture proclaims his infamy in forsaking the land of Israel and its people during the famine.

The sages continue: "When a man dies, the one who feels the loss is his wife, as it is written, 'Elimelech, Naomi's husband, died.'"

A man's death is a double blow to his wife. She loses not only her partner in life, but her breadwinner as well. The orphans will support themselves if they are old enough, or else the court will appoint a guardian to provide for them. But who will support the widow that dwells alone in poverty and is embarrassed to ask for help, especially if she is the widow of a rich man?

Thus when Naomi later returned to the land of Israel, she went hungry rather than go out to pick in the fields. Only Ruth, who was unknown in the land, went out to glean. Accordingly, the Talmud says: "A man's death is only to his wife."

Likewise, since a man or a woman alone is only half a body, a wife's death mainly affects her husband. "When a man loses his wife, his world darkens, his steps shorten, and his counsel disappears." Because women were graced with an extra measure of insight, a husband consults his wife and becomes wise through her words. And a widower therefore has lost not only his helpmate, but his source of counsel as well.

The loss of a wife is likened to the destruction of the Holy Temple. Like the Temple, a wife is a source of light and happiness, well-being and peace. A man without a wife is a man without well-being, without happiness, without peace.

In this case particularly, it is emphasized that the loss of Elimelech affected only his wife. Since he had cared only for himself and his family, and not for other people, his death was a loss only to his family.

How far-reaching are the effects of sin! Until now he had been called "the man Elimelech" (v. 1:2), for he was a great and noble man. Had he died in the land of Israel, the entire nation would have mourned the passing of a prince. Having left his people, however, he was now only "Naomi's husband," and was mourned only by his wife.

Another interpretation is that Elimelech remained Naomi's husband even in death; she did not remarry. A woman of valor who "paid him good and not evil all the days of her life" (Proverbs 31:12), she remained true to him to the end of her own life.

But a subtle change took place. Previously Machlon and Kilyon had been identified as "his sons"; now they are called "her sons." And she herself would no longer be identified with him.

It is stressed that now, too, Naomi remained the respected mother of her two sons. Although the father had died, the sons continued to honor their mother as they had done when he was living.

"She was left"—like the leftovers of the meal offering (Talmud). Elimelech's death is compared to the burning of the handful of flour on the altar. Although most of the flour remains, it is called שְׁיָרֵי מְנָחוֹת, remnants of the meal offering. Similarly, although three members of his family remained, they are called remnants.

Naomi, too, deserved to share Elimelech's fate, for death had been decreed against the entire family. But by God's mercy "she was left" alive. In the merit of her noble deeds her sons were spared for ten years and her own life was saved.

Similarly, our sages teach that death had been decreed against all four sons of Aaron, but prayer by Moses was able to annul half the decree. Nadav and Avihu perished, and of Elazar and Itamar, who were spared, the scripture said, similarly, that they were the sons of Aaron "who were left" (Leviticus 10:12).

She escaped death, but not suffering. The Targum translates: "she was left a widow, and her sons orphans." The entire family was stricken, each in a different way.

Upon leaving the land of Israel, Naomi had been pregnant; in Moab she miscarried. Thus she was to say later, "I went out full, and empty has the Lord returned me" (v. 1:21). She was left with only two children, and even of these she was to become bereft.

Our sages teach: "The All-Merciful does not begin to execute punishment by taking lives." First He strikes at the sinner's property, and he begins by inflicting light losses. If the sinner does not repent, He then goes on to harsher measures. This is made evident in the case of Job. First he was stricken with the death of his cattle and asses, then of his sheep and camels.

Similarly, Machlon and Kilyon first lost their horses, horses being used only for riding but not for carrying burdens; then their donkeys, which are used for both; and finally their camels, which are the most valuable animals. When they still did not repent, God took their lives.

Punishment of Machlon and Kilyon came gradually, in stages. Elimelech's death, on the other hand, came suddenly; it was not preceded by lesser misfortunes. For the sons had merely failed to return to the land of Israel, but he had actively removed the family from the Holy Land.

Moreover, by fleeing from the responsibility of feeding the poor and hungry, Elimelech showed no mercy for others. Therefore, measure for measure, God showed him no mercy, and struck him down suddenly.

Elimelech had cherished his money more than his life. "Happy is he who gives wisely to the poor," David would declare. For "on the day of evil, God will save him" (Psalms 41:2)—by striking first at his wealth. But Elimelech had not been generous to the poor.

Elimelech had sought to lead a pleasant life and ignored the suffering of others. So he lost all his wealth and died alone, mourned only by his immediate family. And after his death, both his sons died.

The scripture teaches that a man's efforts are of no avail against a divine decree. Elimelech fled to Moab to find a haven from famine; instead, in Moab he and his sons met their deaths.

After Elimelech's sudden death for leaving the land of Israel, Naomi remained with her two sons, and they could have saved themselves further suffering by returning to the Holy Land. Instead, they added to their sins. Now that their father was dead, they took Moabite wives without first converting them. Although they lived in Moab for ten years, in all that time they did not repent.

1:4 וַיִּשְׂאוּ לָהֶם נָשִׁים מֹאֲבִיּוֹת שֵׁם הָאַחַת עָרְפָּה וְשֵׁם הַשֵּׁנִית רוּת וַיֵּשְׁבוּ שָׁם כְּעֶשֶׂר שָׁנִים:

They took for themselves in marriage Moabite women. The name of one was Orpah, and the name of the other was Ruth. And they lived there about ten years.

Living among gentiles leads to assimilation, and Machlon and Kilyon assimilated. Their father had brought them to Moab, and the result was that they married Moabite women.

During his lifetime, his sons did not dare take Moabite wives. Elimelech would never have allowed it. But after he died, his sons intermarried. Similarly, notes the Talmud, Solomon refrained from marrying the daughter of Pharaoh as long as his teacher, Shimi ben Gera, was living.

A contributing factor in the family's downfall was their haughtiness. Elimelech, as his name implies ("let kingship come to me"), had aspired to kingship, Naomi was proud of her good deeds, Machlon and Kilyon were prestigious Ephratites. Pride in their accomplishments and in their lineage clouded their judgment and caused them to sin.

In accordance with their stature, God was severe in judging them, because more is expected of great men than of ordinary people.

Some say they died because they were not careful regarding the laws of *leket, shikechah* and *peah*, which require a landowner to leave part of his field and its produce to the needy. Withholding that which the Holy Scripture has designated as "gifts to the poor" is a sin punishable by death, because robbing the poor causes them to die of starvation.

The story is told of a poor woman who sent her two sons to glean in a nearby field, but the owner chased them away. All day the mother waited for them to return home with some food, and when finally they returned, empty-handed, the boys buried their heads in their mother's lap and all three died. Thereupon God ordained, measure for measure, that one who robs the poor pays with his life, as it is written, "For the Lord will take up their cause and despoil of life those that despoil them" (Proverbs 22:23).

For this reason, the book of Ruth is read in the harvest season, on the festival of Shavuoth (Pentecost). We are warned to faithfully fulfill these commandments of giving to the poor, exactly as God has commanded, lest we be stricken as Elimelech's family was.

Abandoning the poor of Israel was bad enough, but now they went so far as to marry Moabite women. The younger brother Kilyon married Orpah, and he was followed by the older brother Machlon, who married Ruth. Thus here Orpah is mentioned first, and the scripture later says, "Ruth the Moabite, wife of Machlon" (v. 4:10).

The Torah expressly forbids a Jew to marry a Moabite or an Ammonite even after conversion. However, Machlon and Kilyon correctly surmised that the prohibition extended only to the men of Moab and Ammon and not to the women. After all, they reasoned, there must be a reason why God had commanded Israel not to war against Ammon and Moab.

The women were excluded from the prohibition because of the two "pearls" that would issue from these two nations. They were Ruth the Moabite, great-grandmother of David, and Naamah the Ammonite, mother of Solomon's successor, Rechavam.

Machlon and Kilyon reasoned correctly but acted wrongly. The law of "a Moabite, not a Moabitess; an Ammonite, not an Ammonitess" (the law that Ammonite and Moabite women were acceptable for marriage as converts) had been forgotten in Israel, and Machlon and Kilyon had no way of knowing that their marriages were not a transgression of Torah law.

Usually the older brother marries first. Here, however, the order was reversed because they married two sisters. The younger brother married the older sister, Orpah, and then the older brother married the younger sister, Ruth. This was a practice designed to increase offspring. Machlon and Kilyon, expecting to be forebears of a royal dynasty, were eager to increase their seed.

Some say that Orpah is mentioned first so that in the verse her name would appear closer to the term "Moabite women," thus stressing Orpah's greater attachment to her nation. Ruth's name comes later in the verse to show that she longed to separate from the Moabite people.

The Midrash teaches that Ruth and Orpah were not converted before their marriage. That is why they are called here "Moabite women," and why Naomi later told them to return to their mother's homes (v. 1:8), and why they retained their original non-Jewish names. The Talmud says: They did not have them convert and immerse; nor had yet the exclusion of women from the prohibition against accepting converts from Ammon and Moab been established as law.

The Torah does not recognize a marriage between a Jew and a gentile, yet the verse says וַיִּשְׂאוּ (vayisu), "they took in marriage." This expression is the one used to describe intermarriage in the book of Ezra. It has the alternate meaning of "raised," that is, they raised their eyes to gentile women.

The Zohar identifies Ruth as the daughter of Eglon, king of Moab. After her father died, she married Machlon, and in her husband's house she learned the ways of Judaism. But her conversion came only later, when she left Moab with Naomi.

The scripture stresses that Machlon and Kilyon married "for themselves," that is, to suit their own fancy. Their mother protested, but they did not heed her.

Nevertheless, it was not for marrying Moabites that Machlon and Kilyon were punished, but for remaining in Moab ten years.

Some say that they did convert the women, and the marriages were arranged properly. This is indicated by the term וַיִּשְׂאוּ, which is one of the proper terms for marriage (nezuin, נשואין), and appears here for the very reason that it also means "they raised." Through marriage with Machlon and Kilyon, the women were raised to such eminence that through them the monarchy of David could now arise.

However, Orpah (עָרְפָּה) was to turn her back (*oreph*, עֹרֶף) on her mother-in-law. Ruth (רוּת) did not follow her example, but saw (*ra'atah*, רָאֲתָה) through her mother-in-law's words and clung to her. Whereupon it was decreed that Orpah's descendants would fall by the hand of Ruth's descendants. This decree came true when the sons of Harafah (2 Samuel 21:16ff.), whom our sages identify as Orpah, battled David's warriors and fell by the hand of David and his men (2 Samuel 21:22).

Ruth, as her name indicates, possessed many virtues. Implied by the numerical equivalent, *gematriya*, of the name Ruth (=606) is that she was not content to observe only the seven Noachide laws required of a gentile. She accepted an additional 606 Torah precepts (*mizvoth*, מצות), and as a full-fledged Jew kept all 613 *mitzvoth*.

By cleaving to the Jewish people, she inherited (ירת in Aramaic) the best of this world and the house of David. She became the ancestress of David, "who saturated (*r'vah*, רוה) God with songs and praises" (Talmud).

Pure as a dove (תור, רות reversed), she was in awe before God and was wary of sin, and it was fitting that she married Machlon, whose name means forgiveness.

According to an opinion stated in Zohar Chadash, before her marriage she converted and her name was changed to Ruth.

Machlon was forgiven, and his name was perpetuated through Ruth. But Kilyon's name was obliterated, because he was the first to sin in marrying a Moabite. One of the very worst transgressions is to pave a sinful path for others to follow.

Time passed, and the brief sojourn envisioned by Elimelech turned into ten years. According to the Targum's rendering of the verse, the brothers attained important positions in Moab and were reluctant to leave. Another reason given is that the famine in the land of Israel would last ten years, and that the Israelites would look to Elimelech to sustain them during the entire decade. So they deliberately stayed away for ten years.

The number ten alludes to the ten exhortations in the Torah to give charity, which Elimelech's family ignored by living in Moab ten years.

Elimelech's family had gained nothing by fleeing the land of Israel. The wealth they had been afraid to dispense as charity was lost in Moab. And while the rest of their people were enduring ten years of famine in *Eretz Yisrael*, his family was enduring an equivalent ten years of poverty and want in Moab.

Although Elimelech died immediately after coming to Moab, he died at a ripe old age and fully righteous, as his name implies. Not so his sons, as their names convey.

The scripture further accents that Machlon and Kilyon had no children during their ten years of marriage, yet they did not divorce their wives.

1:5 וַיָּמֻתוּ גַם־שְׁנֵיהֶם מַחְלוֹן וְכִלְיוֹן וַתִּשָּׁאֵר הָאִשָּׁה מִשְּׁנֵי יְלָדֶיהָ וּמֵאִישָׁהּ:

Then the two of them, Machlon and Kilyon, also died; and the woman was left [bereft] of her children and her husband.

Now they were no longer the titled Ephratites of Bethlehem, Judah, but merely "Machlon and Kilyon." Because they had spurned and forsaken the land of divine choice, they lost their previous eminence.

Elimelech was punished at once upon coming to Moab. His sons died ten years later for not having protested their departure and for not having returned.

As already noted, Naomi was pregnant when she left Bethlehem. And the word "also" refers not only to the loss of her husband, but the loss as well of the child that she carried.

According to Targum Yonathan, the verse also conveys that Machlon and Kilyon died a double death, for they died in a land that lacked the sanctity of *Eretz Yisrael*. Similarly, when Jeremiah prophesied about the High Priest Pashchur that he would be led captive to Babylon and die there, he said to him, "You shall die, and there you shall be buried" (Jeremiah 20:6). This implies that whoever dies outside the land of Israel suffers a double death.

(The middle letter *vav* (ו) of וימותו conveys that the death of Machlon and Kilyon came about after six other deaths had occurred as a warning. First their horses died, then their donkeys, their camels, the camel drivers, the sheep, and the cattle. They failed to heed the warning, and finally they, too, died.

Naomi could have averted these additional misfortunes by returning as soon as her husband died. Instead, וַתִּשָּׁאֵר הָאִשָּׁה, "the woman remained."

At the time of their death they were grown men, but to the mother they were still "her two children." Moreover, this conveys that their final illness made them helpless as children, whom Naomi tended like a mother caring for her little ones.

And when they died, the loss was not to their wives, as the scripture might have been expected to indicate, but to their mother.

With the death of her sons, the death of her husband now became total, for she was left without seed from him. Accordingly, she was "left bereft," as a wife that is bereft of her husband.

Hence she was no longer Naomi, "the pleasant one," but "the woman." As she was to say later, "Call me not Naomi, for the Almighty has dealt very bitterly with me" (v. 1:20).

After the loss of Elimelech, she had found comfort in her sons. The present loss thus brought back to her afresh the entire tragedy.

Similarly, we find that when Jacob was confronted with a new misfortune, he was reminded of the earlier tragedy. "Joseph is not, Simeon is not, and you will also take Benjamin? All these have come upon me" (Genesis 42:36).

As with Jacob, all the tragedies Naomi had suffered in the past ten years seemed to converge on her at once. The compounded loss of her unborn child, of her husband, and finally of her two childless sons, crushed Naomi. She became ill with grief over the destruction of her entire family. "The woman was left"—sick, barren, broken.

The death of her husband took on a new finality, for now there were no heirs to perpetuate his name and to found a royal dynasty. Naomi was left with her prophetic dream of sovereignty shattered.

Until now she had thought that the royal line would begin in Moab. But with her husband and her only offspring dead by divine decree, there was no purpose in remaining there any longer.

In anticipation, however, the verse hints that although she was now a childless widow, alone in her grief, she was not entirely alone. She was left bereft "of her two children and of her husband," but she was not abandoned by her daughters-in-law. Orpah and Ruth remained at her

Ruth 1

side, and when she rose to return to the land of Israel, they made preparations to accompany her.

1:6 וַתָּקָם הִיא וְכַלֹּתֶיהָ וַתָּשָׁב מִשְּׂדֵי מוֹאָב כִּי שָׁמְעָה בִּשְׂדֵה מוֹאָב כִּי־פָקַד יְהֹוָה אֶת־עַמּוֹ לָתֵת לָהֶם לָחֶם:

She rose, with her daughters-in-law, and returned from the Fields of Moab. For she heard in the Fields of Moab that God remembered His people to give them bread.

It is made clear that not the women but the men had prevented the family from returning to the land of Israel. No sooner had Machlon and Kilyon died, then their womenfolk rose to go back.

There is a significant contrast between the present singular form: "she rose ... returned ... heard" (ותקם ... ותשב ... שמעה), and the plural form of the following verse: "... and her *two* daughters-in-law ... went" (pl. ותלכנה). At first she and her daughters-in-law went as one, but then it became apparent that the daughters-in-law were headed in two different directions.

Additionally, the verse conveys that the decision to return to the land of Israel was made as soon as they "rose," that is, as soon as they had literally risen from sitting on the ground during the seven days of mourning for the deceased. Thus we find, similarly, that at the episode of the golden calf, the Israelites demanded of Aaron, "Arise and make for us gods," upon which our sages elaborate: Aaron was sitting in mourning over the slaying of Chur and the seventy elders.

Another interpretation is that Naomi rose from the illness that grief had brought on.

Her decision made, Naomi rose earlier than is customary. She did not want to be detained by well-meaning neighbors who would insist on a proper send-off, as befits a great woman. Having heard that the famine was over, she did not want to lose a minute.

Naomi wisely realized that if she discussed her plans with her daughters-in-law, they would plead with her to remain. So she kept silent until the actual time to leave had arrived, and then simply rose to go. Her daughters-in-law then hurriedly joined her.

Although the present verse says that "she ... returned," it does not mean that she actually returned, for the next verse states that "she left the place." At this point she had only resolved to return. God, however, rewards good intentions as if they were accomplished deeds, and the verse says "she returned."

These words ("she returned") accent, moreover, that Naomi went back empty-handed. Of all Elimelech's tents and servants and herds and camels and great wealth, including the ten fields that he had acquired in Moab (Talmud), nothing was left. Thus she was to say later, "I went out full, and empty has the Lord returned me" (v. 1:21).

What prompted her return was the news that the famine had come to an end. We are informed that she was told, "God has remembered His people," which means that she heard the glad tidings from itinerant peddlers from *Eretz Yisrael*. Alternately, she reasoned that if people were once again buying the peddlers' luxury wares, they must already have bread in the house.

According to Targum Yonathan, an angel appeared to Naomi in the field to inform her that the famine was over.

Although Naomi had just risen from her sickbed and was penniless, she left at once. She did not wait for her neighbors to provide her with food for the journey, but placed her trust in God to bring her home safely. Thus she repented for having despaired of God saving Israel from the famine.

Another opinion is that Naomi did not actually hear any news, but on her own understood that the famine had ended. Moab, too, had to some extent been affected by the famine, and when she now saw the fields of Moab newly covered with lush grass and flowers, she knew that the land of Israel must be blooming once more.

Naomi realized, moreover, that only through the land of Israel does God bless the other nations with abundance. "For she heard ... that God remembered His people"—i.e., in the land of Israel—"to give them"—the Moabites—"bread."

It is implied that God remembered His people with rain, since the resulting crops would then "give them bread." So it was that by the time Naomi actually returned, the barley was being harvested.

This also indicates that this turn of events was sudden. The famine was to have lasted longer, but in the merit of the righteous Boaz, it ended at this time.

Naomi had been informed that the people had not yet repented of the injustice and strife that had precipitated the famine. So the rain came not because Israel deserved it, but because God in His mercy remembered

His people. Armed with this knowledge, she dared to return to the Holy Land despite the fact that God was still dealing with her in strict justice rather than mercy. She trusted that among her own people she, too, would be affected by the divine mercy that was extended to them for having remained in the Holy Land during the famine.

Naomi was like that poor guest at the inn who would not join the crowds that came there to eat and drink, because he could not afford the lavish food. But one day the innkeeper made a feast for all his guests for which no payment was required, whereupon the poor guest, too, ate and drank along with the rest.

If Naomi had heard that God ended the famine because the people were worthy of it, she would not have dared to return. But as He was providing them with bread out of mercy rather than justice, she came.

At another time in the future, in the days of the prophet Joel, Israel was also stricken with famine. But then the famine ended because "God was zealous for His land, and pitied His people" (Joel 2:18). In the days of the judges, "God remembered His people." Although they were not entirely repentant, He gave them bread because they had remained in the Holy Land during the famine and relied on God to save them from starvation.

1:7 וַתֵּצֵא מִן־הַמָּקוֹם אֲשֶׁר הָיְתָה־שָׁמָּה וּשְׁתֵּי כַלֹּתֶיהָ עִמָּהּ וַתֵּלַכְנָה בַדֶּרֶךְ לָשׁוּב אֶל־אֶרֶץ יְהוּדָה׃

She left the place where she had been, and her two daughters-in-law were with her. They went on the road back to the land of Judah.

The previous verse recounted that Naomi "rose, with her daughters-in-law, and returned from the Fields of Moab." After interjecting, however, that the famine had ended, the narrative resumes by repeating that "she left the place where she had been."

These two verses are similar but not identical. As previously noted, the first verse indicates that the three women had initially risen as one to return; the second, that en route "her *two* daughters-in-law" turned out to be of *two* minds. Orpah accompanied Naomi out of politeness, but Ruth longed to cleave to her.

Others say that when Naomi rose to return, she assumed that her daughters-in-law were merely seeing her off. Now that they had crossed the border and still "her . . . two daughters-in-law were with her," she realized that they intended to go "to the land of Judah," there to join the Jewish people.

The reason for the journey was as much to escape the place of their suffering ("she left the place where she had been") as to see the longed-for Holy Land ("They went . . . back to the land of Judah").

The Talmud teaches: "The *tzaddik* (righteous man) of a city is its radiance and light, its glory and praise. When he departs, the city's radiance and light, glory and praise, depart with him." For the *tzaddik* influences the people about him to become righteous.

Thus the scripture records that "Jacob went out of Beersheba" (Genesis 28:10), even as it says here that Naomi "left the place where she had been," to indicate that their departures noticeably affected the places they left behind.

While Naomi was living in Moab the decadent Moabites curbed their immorality. Now that she left, the Moabites fell back to their previous practices, as evidenced by what later happened to Orpah. The glory of Moab departed with Naomi.

Of all places in the land of Israel, Naomi returned "to the land of Judah." Although a person who has suffered bad fortune is ashamed to return to his hometown, Naomi accepted her suffering with love and willingly returned to Bethlehem in order to atone for leaving the Holy Land.

Some say that Naomi, ashamed to face the people she had deserted during the famine, would have preferred to go where she was unknown. Nevertheless, she returned to her hometown because it afforded the best chances of supporting her daughters-in-law.

The three women, anxious to get to the Holy Land, immediately "went on the road." That is, they set out alone on the road, without waiting to travel in the safety of a caravan.

To minimize the danger, they took "the road," the main thoroughfare, avoiding deserted side roads. Moreover, it is indicated that they clung together to avoid seclusion with men, for they were on their way to the holy "land of Judah."

In their eagerness to get there, "they went"—they walked without stopping to rest.

Our sages observe that they literally walked "on the road." Too poor to buy riding animals or even shoes to protect their feet, they walked barefoot, hurting their feet on the road. According to one interpretation, they went on foot because in their eager haste they also traveled on the festival, when riding is prohibited.

Every step they took was with the specific intention of going "to the land of Judah." God therefore rewarded them for every step (Talmud).

As they walked, they studied the laws of conversion. For Ruth and Orpah were on their way "to . . . Judah" also in another sense, that is, to embrace the faith that derives its name from "Judah."

"When a gentile wishes to convert," teaches the Talmud, "he is to be turned away with the left hand and drawn closer with the right." Naomi thus drew her daughters-in-law close by teaching them that so precious were converts in God's eyes that His Torah warns no less than forty-eight times against distressing a convert. [On the other hand, she attempted to turn them away, as the following verses recount.]

1:8 וַתֹּאמֶר נָעֳמִי לִשְׁתֵּי כַלֹּתֶיהָ לֵכְנָה שֹּׁבְנָה אִשָּׁה לְבֵית אִמָּהּ יעשה (יַעַשׂ קרי) יְהוָה עִמָּכֶם חֶסֶד כַּאֲשֶׁר עֲשִׂיתֶם עִם־הַמֵּתִים וְעִמָּדִי:

Naomi said to her two daughters-in-law: "Go, return each to her mother's house. May the Lord deal kindly with you, as you have dealt with the deceased and with me."

Even after their husbands died, Ruth and Orpah continued to relate to Naomi as their mother-in-law, and she still saw in them "her . . . daughters-in-law."

The three of them were already "on the road back to the land of Judah" (v. 7), when Naomi turned to Ruth and Orpah and told them to return. She had waited until then because only then did she realize that they intended to travel with her the whole way.

At first she had thought that her two daughters-in-law "were with her" (v. 6) only to see her off. But when they reached "the road that led back to Judah" (v. 7), Ruth and Orpah showed no signs of turning back. Instead, they adjusted their clothing [in keeping with standards of modesty in Judah], thus revealing their intentions.

Another interpretation is that Naomi had thought they were coming with her to the land of Israel to collect the marriage settlements (*kethuboth*, כתובות) to which as widows they were entitled. When, however, they renounced their claims, as our sages reveal, she understood that they wanted to join the Jewish people, and she tried to dissuade them.

To test their determination, Naomi let them taste the hardships of the journey before telling them to "Go, return."

The test revealed the difference between her "two" daughters-in-law. Ruth remained steadfast and Orpah returned.

Even before testing them, Naomi had perceived Ruth's purity of heart and felt closer to her than to Orpah. For the sake of peace, however, she spoke to the two equally and urged them both to go back. Preferential treatment was therefore not a factor in Ruth staying and Orpah leaving.

The form "go, return" is significant in this regard. To Orpah, who did not truly wish to convert, she said simply "go," that is, go back to Moab. To Ruth, who ardently desired to join the Jewish people, Naomi said "return"—go back to your decision.

"Return to your mothers' houses," she advised, "for I have no house and no means of supporting you. I may have been like a mother to you; but a real mother will treat you better than a good mother-in-law.

"Nor be afraid that your mothers will reject you for marrying Jews. God will deal kindly with you and see that you are welcome."

Naomi told them to go "each to her mother's house," rather than the father's, for a number of reasons:

(1) Gentiles then traced their descent through their mothers.

(2) If Ruth and Orpah had displeased their parents by marrying out of their people, their mothers, being by nature more merciful, would more readily forgive and accept them.

(3) Generally it is the mother who stays home, while the father goes out to work. And it is the mother who would care for a widowed daughter and prepare her dowry.

According to our sages, Ruth and Orpah were daughters of Eglon, king of Moab, evidently by differently wives, for Naomi told each to return to *her* mother's house.

By telling them "go, return," Naomi was in fact offering various options. One was that they accompany her to Bethlehem and then return.

Then again [according to the opinion that before marrying Machlon and Kilyon, Ruth and Orpah had converted]—they could "go" to Moab as Jews or "return" to the idolatry of their mothers' homes. [This she said in order to test them.] In either case, she told them, God would repay them for the kindness they had extended to the deceased and to her.

However, God's kindness would be fuller if they remained faithful than if they returned to idolatry. This is conveyed by the expression "may [He] deal." Although the Hebrew original is written in full (ya'ase, יעשה), in pronunciation it is truncated (ya'as, יעש) [as if the letter heh ה, (numerical value 5) was missing. God would deal differently with them if they remained faithful to the Five Books of Moses, than if they did not.]

If they turned back, God would reward them in full for the forty paces they had accompanied Naomi thus far. This is conveyed by the unexpected masculine ending of "with you" (עִמָּכֶם) instead of the grammatically proper עִמָּכֶן). The numerical value of the final letter (ם) is forty.

And if they cleaved to the Jewish people, God's kindness would culminate five generations later, in the golden era of Ruth's great-great-grandson King Solomon. This is likewise alluded to by the letter ה in the written form יעשה. The five generations are Boaz, Obed, Ishai, David, Solomon.

The reward for cleaving to Naomi is further hinted at in the word עִמָּדִי ("with me"), an acronym of Obed (ע of עבד), the Messiah (מ of משיח), David (ד of דוד), Ishai (י of ישי)—all of whom would descend from Ruth.

Naomi continued: "Do not fear that by leaving me now you will forfeit the merit of your past kindness. Your reward will remain intact; God will deal kindly with you as you have dealt with the deceased and with me."

Nor would they lose their reward by being far away from Naomi. God, Who is "desirous of kindness" (Micah 7:18), would requite their kindness wherever they went. For kindness [by man is imitative of the divine attribute of kindness—*chesed*, and] is one of the pillars that hold up the world, as it is written: "The world is build on kindness" (Psalms 89:3).

Naomi prayed, "May the Lord deal kindly with you," because the convert's lot in this world is not a happy one, since he must atone for his past sins.

Here, too, Naomi tested their determination to convert. By pronouncing the term יעשה as if it were written with one letter missing, she hinted that a convert is shown less kindness than a born Jew. If they replied: "We know, and we are not worthy of that other kindness," their sincerity would be made evident.

In her bitterness, Naomi likened kindness to her with kindness to the dead—"as you have dealt with the deceased and with me." Both could rightly be termed "true kindness" (חסד של אמת), that is, kindness without hope of reciprocation. "So poor am I," she said, "that I can no more repay your kindness than can the dead.

"But," she added, "God will pay you back by giving you rest, each in the home of her husband" (v. 9).

Naomi praised Ruth and Orpah for dealing kindly "with the deceased" by being good wives to Machlon and Kilyon and, according to the Targum, by refusing to remarry after they died.

Our sages say that they provided the shrouds and paid for the burials, although widows are not legally obligated to do so. Naomi therefore blessed them: "May God deal kindly with you as you have dealt with the deceased. Just as you clothed the deceased in clean shrouds, so in the World to Come will God clothe you in the pure souls of *tzaddikim*, to enable you to appear and bow down before Him."

Naomi praised them for their kindness to her also after her sons died—"with the deceased and [afterwards] with me." They had mourned for them, says the Midrash, and they cried "with me."

Moreover, they gave up their marriage settlements, which they were entitled to collect from the family's fields in Bethlehem. In a magnificent act of kindness, they left all the family property to Naomi.

An alternate interpretation is that Naomi had co-signed their *kethuboth*. Yet, when her sons died, they did not collect from her, but lived with her until their money ran out. Then they left Moab.

"By continuing to deal kindly with me even after my sons died," said Naomi, "you showed that your kindness to me while they were living was always sincere, and not because of your husbands."

Naomi addressed them in the masculine form (עִמָּכֶם, "with you") to commend their manly determination and strength of character. Hence they could not be suspected of ulterior motives. The acts of kindness they had done for the living and the dead testified to their purity of heart and their love of God and man.

1:9 יִתֵּן יְהוָה לָכֶם וּמְצֶאןָ מְנוּחָה אִשָּׁה בֵּית אִישָׁהּ וַתִּשַּׁק לָהֶן וַתִּשֶּׂאנָה קוֹלָן וַתִּבְכֶּינָה:

"God grant that you will find rest, each in the house of her husband." Then she kissed them, and they raised their voice and wept.

After Naomi assured her daughters-in-law that their kindness would be requited in full by God dealing "kindly with you as you have dealt with the deceased and with me" (v. 8), she added: "In return for giving up your marriage settlements, may God grant you wealth. And in return for bringing to rest your deceased husbands, may each of you find rest in the house of her new husband."

Proper burial is an act of kindness that affords repose to the body and peace to the soul, as it is written: "He will come in peace, they will rest on their couches" (Isaiah 57:2).

Recall in this regard Jacob's bitter lament—"A wild beast has devoured him! Joseph has been torn apart!" (Genesis 37:33)—when he thought that Joseph had died without burial.

And it is fitting that in return for properly burying the dead, Ruth and Orpah would find personal tranquility in remarriage.

According to the Targum, Naomi said, "May God grant you wealth in the full measure of your kindness. Your wealth will attract distinguished suitors, and among them you will select husbands to make you happy."

Naomi said, "God grant." She wished them prosperity from the bounteous hand of God rather than from the niggardly hands of mortals.

To Naomi's words, "You will find rest, each in the house of her husband," our sages relate the teaching that a woman is never content except in her husband's home. The wealthy widow living in a palace and the pampered daughter in her father's house may enjoy material comfort. But only in her husband and children does a woman find fulfillment and peace of mind.

In wishing them "rest, each in the house of her husband," Naomi was also praying that they have the peace and security of owning their own homes, instead of living in rented dwellings together with their in-laws. For rarely do a mother-in-law and daughter-in-law live peacefully under one roof as Naomi had lived with Ruth and Orpah.

Another in Naomi's position would have blamed her suffering on her daughters-in-law. She, however, grieved over their suffering—their poverty, their childlessness, and their widowhood. And she wholeheartedly prayed that God would bless them with wealth, happy marriages, and children, and spare them further tragedy.

"If your first marriages were ill-fated because my sons married you to suit their whims," she said to them, "may your second marriages be ordained by God. You will then find contentment."

Although our sages teach that first rather than second marriages are ordained before birth, second marriages are decreed according to a person's deeds. And on account of their kindness "with the deceased and with me," Naomi assured them that their second marriages would be happy ones.

She prayed that her barren daughters-in-law would succeed in raising a family—the mark of the mainstay of the home, as it is written: "He sets up the mainstay of the house; the mother of the children is happy" (Psalms 113:9).

At the mention of marriage, however, Ruth and Orpah recalled their dead husbands, and they "raised their voice and wept."

On another level of meaning, Naomi's blessings were prophetic regarding each of her daughters-in-law.

In the merit of the forty steps that Orpah had accompanied Naomi, her descendant Goliath would be spared for forty days before being slain by David. This is conveyed by the masculine form of "(to) you" (לָכֶם rather than לָכֵן). The letter *mem* (ם) corresponds to the number forty.

Ruth would live to see her descendants David and Solomon sitting on the throne of Israel. The letters of לָכֶם may be rearranged to spell מֶלֶךְ—king.

This indicates, accordingly, that Ruth, who derived her [spiritual] descent from Judah's wife Tamar, would "find rest in the house" of Judah's descendant Boaz. It would only be a momentary haven, however, as hinted at by the missing final letter ה of וּמְצֶאןָ. Boaz died the very night of their wedding.

From Ruth and Boaz would descend Solomon, of whom God said, "He will be a man of rest, and I shall give him rest from all his enemies around him ... He will build a House for My name" (1 Chronicles 22:9-10). And the *Beit HaMikdash* (Holy Temple) is the resting place of the Divine Presence.

From Ruth and Boaz, too, would descend the Messiah. He will usher in an era when the Jewish people will be gathered, never to be exiled again. Israel will thus find rest in the land of God, even as a woman finds "rest ... in the house of her husband." Thus the prophet says: "At that time you will call Me *my Husband*; you will no longer call Me *my Master*" (Hosea 2:18).

Moreover, it is indicated that since the Third Temple will be built by God Himself, it will aptly be called His House, hence "the house of her husband."

Ruth would be the mother of prophets as well as kings, and this, too, is conveyed by the word "rest." Thus our sages deduce from the verse, "Seraiah (שַׂר י־ה, prince of God), the prince of rest" (Jeremiah 51:59), that Baruch ben Neriyah attained prophecy.

Having blessed her daughters-in-law, "she kissed them," just as Isaac had kissed his son Jacob upon blessing him (Genesis 27:27). The kiss symbolizes transfer of the blessing by binding together the souls of the one giving and the one receiving the blessing.

Some authorities write that the kiss of a *tzaddik* awakens the soul of a pure person from its slumber. But if the person is impure, the kiss draws the sparks of holiness out of him, and he remains without a basis of existence. After Naomi's kiss, accordingly, "they raised their voice (singular) and wept." [They did not weep together, i.e., for the same reason; each wept separately.] Ruth wept out of longing for God, Naomi's kiss having aroused her desire to cleave to Him. And Orpah wept over her downfall, for she realized that she had lost her sparks of holiness.

1:10

וַתֹּאמַרְנָה־לָּהּ כִּי־אִתָּךְ נָשׁוּב לְעַמֵּךְ:

They said to her, "No, with you shall we return to your people."

When Naomi kissed them farewell, Ruth and Orpah protested that they would not forsake her, but "with you . . . return to your people."

Although they had never been there, they spoke of returning to Judah. "So strong is our love of Israel," they said, "that going to Judah is like returning home.

"Although you prayed that God should deal kindly with us if we returned to our mothers' home, we trust He will treat us just as kindly if we come with you."

According to the Targum, they were replying to Naomi's advice to "Go, return each to her mother's house" (v. 8). "No, we will not go back to the idols of Moab; we will return with you to the God of Israel."

Although Naomi had warned them that the life of a convert was full of suffering and sadness, they nevertheless insisted on converting.

Their motivations, however, differed. Both Ruth and Orpah had "raised their voice and wept" (v. 9), and both now said, "with you we will return to your people." But Orpah stressed the word אִתָּךְ, "with you"; her wish was to be with Naomi, and to that end she was willing to convert; and Ruth said לְעַמֵּךְ, "to your people." Her primary motive was conversion to Judaism; being with Naomi was secondary.

Furthermore, they insisted on going with Naomi because "with you we shall return to your people." That is, only from her could they receive the necessary instruction preparatory to their conversion.

They also needed Naomi to testify to their sincerity. For if they were suspected of converting because of Israel's new prosperity they would be turned away, as all would-be converts were later turned away during the golden age of King Solomon.

1:11 וַתֹּאמֶר נָעֳמִי שֹׁבְנָה בְנֹתַי לָמָּה תֵלַכְנָה עִמִּי הַעוֹד־לִי בָנִים בְּמֵעַי וְהָיוּ לָכֶם לַאֲנָשִׁים:

Naomi said, "Return, my daughters. Why go with me? Have I more sons in my womb who might be husbands for you?"

Now that Ruth and Orpah had expressed a desire to convert, Naomi tenderly called them "my daughters." She tried to dissuade them, however, suspecting that their desire to convert stemmed from love of her, not love of God. And she pleaded that remaining with her was impossible. The bonds of marriage which had united them were now dissolved by death and could not be renewed, for she had no more sons to give them.

"Why go with me if you insist on converting? Go to a different city in Israel and spare me the pain of seeing my sons' wives married to strangers. And if you want to become Jews because you are like daughters to me—return. I cannot accept such self-sacrifice.

"Nor is it even advisable for you to go with me, if your intention purely is to join the Jewish people. Go to Judah alone, lest you be suspected of converting on my account. For then you would not be accepted as converts.

"Go back to Moab and marry there," she further argued, "for no Israelite men will want to be your husbands. The law permitting marriage with women converts from Moab is not commonly known, and the few who know of it may be afraid to rely on it. Nor will they want to marry women who were childless in a previous marriage.

"And you cannot rely on me. Machlon and Kilyon are dead, my unborn child is dead. Even if I were carrying sons now, after you will have grown old waiting for them to come of age, they might not want to be your husbands.

"Nor could they be your husbands, according to Torah law." Marrying a brother's widow is forbidden except in levirate marriage (*yibum*, יִבּוּם), for the sake of perpetuating the name of the deceased through offspring. Since *yibum* applies, however, only 'if brothers dwell together' (Deuteronomy 25:5), that is, if the two brothers were in this world at the same time, a man born after his brother's death is ineligible for *yibum*, and forbidden to marry his brother's widow.

Naomi therefore said that even if she had sons in her womb now, they could not "be husbands for you."

1:12 שֹׁבְנָה בְנֹתַי לֵכְןָ כִּי זָקַנְתִּי מִהְיוֹת לְאִישׁ כִּי אָמַרְתִּי יֶשׁ־לִי תִקְוָה גַּם הָיִיתִי הַלַּיְלָה לְאִישׁ וְגַם יָלַדְתִּי בָנִים:

"Return, my daughters, go. For I am too old to have a husband. For were I even to say there is hope for me or even if I were to have a husband tonight and I also bore sons..."

For the third time now, Naomi told her daughters-in-law to "return," in keeping with the teaching of our sages that a would-be convert should be turned away three times. If he nevertheless persists, he is then accepted.

Rabbi Yitzchak expounded: A would-be convert is kept away with his left hand and drawn near with the right, as it is written: "My door to the wayfarer I will open; outside a stranger shall not sleep" (Job 31:32). That is, I do not open my door to a stranger—a gentile who comes to convert—as readily as to a wayfarer; but if the stranger persists in knocking, I will not close the door to him.

"If we could all continue to live together," she now urged, "it would be reasonable for you to come with me. But why do so, when ultimately you must marry out of the family and leave me?"

Naomi again called them "my daughters." She felt towards them like a mother who is anxious to see her widowed daughters find husbands, not like a mother-in-law who is angry if her sons' widows remarry.

It was inevitable that they would marry out of the family, she said. She had no other sons for them to marry; "I am too old to have a husband" and bear more children. And it was ludicrous to imagine that in the land of Israel she would suddenly become rejuvenated, immediately find a husband, marry, conceive, and bear not daughters, but sons for both of them to marry.

"Even if I were to become young again," she pursued, "and I married this very night and bore sons, why should you languish in widowhood waiting for them to reach marriageable age?"

According to the opinion that Ruth and Orpah had not converted before marrying Machlon and Kilyon, they could marry Naomi's future sons, as their first marriages were then void by Torah law and the prohibition of marrying a brother's widow would not apply.

It is significant and prophetic that Naomi said, "Return . . . go." For one would in fact return to Judah with her, and the other would go back to Moab.

1:13 הֲלָהֵן תְּשַׂבֵּרְנָה עַד אֲשֶׁר יִגְדָּלוּ הֲלָהֵן תֵּעָגֵנָה לְבִלְתִּי הֱיוֹת לְאִישׁ אַל בְּנֹתַי כִּי־מַר־לִי מְאֹד מִכֶּם כִּי־יָצְאָה בִי יַד־יְהֹוָה:

"Would you wait for them until they are grown? Would you shut yourselves off for them and have no husbands? No, my daughters, for I am very bitter for you [alt: I am more bitter than you]. For the hand of God has gone out against me."

"If you are coming with me in the hope of marrying sons I may yet bear, turn back. For even if you are willing to remain widows until they are of age to marry, by then you will be far too old, and they will not marry you. Besides, ever since Abraham married Sarah, men have married younger women."

Ruth 1

By her use of the feminine form (להן instead of להם), Naomi further reminded them that even if she did bear children, they might, after all, be girls.

Ruth and Orpah might, however, be content to remain widows out of respect to their dead husbands, so she pleaded against it. "I am bitter enough over your past misfortunes. Do not add to my grief by living the rest of your lives in the miseries of widowhood.

"If I myself refuse to remarry, it is because I am broken over the loss of my whole family and all my possessions. My suffering is far more bitter than yours. 'There is no soundness in my flesh because of God's anger; there is no health in my bones because of my sin' (Psalms 38:4). But you are still youthful and vigorous, and can still recover what you have lost."

Naomi thus assured her daughters-in-law that she was not sending them away because she blamed them for her sons' deaths. She blamed only her sins for her misfortunes. Just as Jeremiah was later to proclaim, "The crown is fallen from our heads; woe to us for *we* have sinned" (Jeremiah 5:16), Naomi declared: "The hand of God has gone out against *me*."

This also indicates that her sons had died of the pestilence, the plague the Egyptians called "the hand of God" (Exodus 9:3). Remarkably, although the disease is extremely contagious, it was restricted to her family alone—clear evidence that it was a divine punishment.

Indeed, her suffering had "gone out" of the ordinary. She was smitten not by the finger of God but by His hand, five blows in all: the deaths of her husband, her two sons, and the unborn child, and her extreme destitution. So much misfortune could be due only to her sins.

"By being with me, you, too, have suffered because of the hand of God that has stricken me," said Naomi. "Therefore leave me and go back to Moab, where you will find happiness in remarriage."

1:14 וַתִּשֶּׂנָה קוֹלָן וַתִּבְכֶּינָה עוֹד וַתִּשַּׁק עָרְפָּה לַחֲמוֹתָהּ וְרוּת דָּבְקָה בָּהּ׃

They raised their voice and wept again. Orpah kissed her mother-in-law, but Ruth cleaved to her.

When Naomi first urged them to return to Moab, Orpah and Ruth had "raised (וַיִּשְׂאוּ) their voice and wept" (v. 9). And they continued weeping as they walked, until their strength gave out. Thus the missing letter א here associates וַתִּשֶּׂנָה to תֶּשִׁי, weakness; as in "Of the Rock that begot you, weakness (תֶּשִׁי), and you forgot God, Who bore you" (Deuteronomy 32:18). Such was their exhaustion that they could barely raise their voices.

Naomi's moving plea (vs. 12–13), full of love and concern for their welfare, evoked fresh tears, and "they raised their voice and wept again."

[The singular form ("voice") is significant.] Only Ruth's weeping came from the depths of her being. Orpah's weeping was patently superficial, for she "kissed her mother-in-law" and left. This time (compare v. 9), she did not even wait for a parting kiss from Naomi. This too is conveyed in the incomplete spelling of וַתִּשֶּׂנָה.

Our sages infer that nevertheless, in the merit of the four tears she had shed—[hinted at by the four words (וַתִּשֶּׂנָה קוֹלָן וַתִּבְכֶּינָה עוֹד) that describe the weeping]—four mighty warriors would descend from her. Thus it is written, "These four were born to Harafah in Gat" (2 Samuel 21:22), namely Saf, Madon (Lahmi), Goliath, and Yishbi (ibid: 16, 18, 19, 20, 1 Chronicles 20 ff.).

Ruth truly wept and clung to Naomi out of love. Thus the women of Bethlehem were later to observe: "Your daughter-in-law who loves you, she who is better to you than seven sons, has borne him" (v. 4:15).

Our sages declare: Let the sons of Orpah, who kissed Naomi, fall by the hands of the sons of Ruth, who cleaved to her. And generations after the two sisters-in-law parted ways, the four warriors who came from Orpah were slain by Ruth's great-grandson David and his men (1 Chronicles 20 ff.).

1:15 וַתֹּאמֶר הִנֵּה שָׁבָה יְבִמְתֵּךְ אֶל־עַמָּהּ וְאֶל־אֱלֹהֶיהָ שׁוּבִי אַחֲרֵי יְבִמְתֵּךְ׃

She said, "Behold, your sister-in-law has returned to her people and to her gods; return after your sister-in-law."

Both Ruth and Orpah had declared their intention to convert. Nevertheless, after Naomi told them that she could not arrange for them to marry distinguished men suitable for a king's daughters, Orpah left. In a final test of Ruth's determination to convert, Naomi now told her to follow Orpah's example and go back to Moab.

Ruth 1

"Your sister-in-law came this far out of courtesy and because she was ashamed to leave me," said Naomi, "but now she has returned home. You are also free to depart. Do not feel obligated to remain because Orpah has left."

Another interpretation is that Naomi, thinking she succeeded in persuading Ruth to leave, urged her to hurry and catch up with Orpah ("return after your sister-in-law"), so the two could travel together.

Although Orpah had but returned "to her people," Naomi knew that under their influence she would also return "to her gods." In this regard, the influence of the environment is already noted in the Torah, which warns: "they [idolators] shall not dwell in your midst lest they cause you to sin against Me" (Exodus 23:33).

One who encourages a Jew to worship idols incurs the death penalty. If therefore Naomi told Ruth to return after her sister-in-law who "has returned to her gods," evidently Ruth had not yet converted. Or else, Ruth and Orpah had converted to marry Machlon and Kilyon, but invalidated the conversion by secretly continuing to worship idols.

However, Naomi spoke as she did in order to test Ruth, and she chose her words carefully. She did not actually say, "return to your gods," but "return after your sister-in-law." She accepted Ruth's sincerity of faith, and only urged her to go back to her father's house in Orpah's company.

1:16 וַתֹּאמֶר רוּת אַל־תִּפְגְּעִי־בִי לְעָזְבֵךְ לָשׁוּב מֵאַחֲרָיִךְ כִּי אֶל־אֲשֶׁר
תֵּלְכִי אֵלֵךְ וּבַאֲשֶׁר תָּלִינִי אָלִין עַמֵּךְ עַמִּי וֵאלֹהַיִךְ אֱלֹהָי:

But Ruth said: "Entreat me not to leave you, to return from following after you. Where you go, I will go, and where you lodge, I will lodge; your people are my people, and your God is my God."

When urged to follow the example of Orpah, who returned "to her people and to her gods," Ruth countered: "Your people are my people, and your God is my God."

Naomi had also advised her to return to her mother's house or go to Judah on her own. The first she rejected categorically, declaring, "I will not go back to the idolatry of my mother's house. Your people are my people, and your God is my God." And to the second, upon which

Naomi had a right to insist, she replied: "Entreat me (תפגעי) not to leave you, to return from following after you."

The expression תִּפְגְּעִי can also mean strike a blow, and thus Ruth conveyed to Naomi that she was stung by the insinuation that she was only accompanying her out of politeness. "In coming with you I have no ulterior motive, not even to collect my marriage settlement in Bethlehem. Wherever you go, be it Bethlehem or elsewhere, I will go.

"Your sharp words will not turn me away. Even if you tell me black is white, I will follow you and obey you.

"Nor can you frighten me away by implying that the hand of God that has gone out against you may also strike me if I cleave to you.

"Even if I remarry, I will not leave you. Nothing, not the land, nor differences of nationality, religion, or custom, will separate me from you.

"You wished us to find rest in the houses of our husbands, but I am not looking for peace and security; I would rather be a wanderer casting about for my lodging with you, than live in the palace of a king.

"And if you do not let me come with you, I will go alone to Judah to convert. Where you go—i.e.; to Judah—there will I go; for your God and your people are mine. And our paths must eventually join, for our goals are the same."

Leaving Naomi was for Ruth like forsaking the Torah; by the seemingly redundant phrase, "to return from following after you," she indicated that with every step she might take away from Naomi, the distance between them would double. Similarly our sages teach: When a person departs from the Torah, the Torah departs from him, hence doubling the separation between them.

Naomi had instructed her in the commandments, and Ruth now committed herself to fulfill them. "Your people are my people" was her acceptance of the laws between man and his fellow; "your God is my God" relates to the laws between man and God.

Our sages expound: "Your people are my people"—these are punishments and warnings [of the Torah which Ruth now accepted as binding]. "Your God is my God"—these are the other precepts.

Another implication: "Your people are my people" who will take me away from idolatry; "your God is my God" who will reward me for my labor. Ruth thus expressed her belief in reward and punishment.

Naomi instructed her with particular care in the laws of the Sabbath, for Sabbath observance unequivocally attests to belief in God as Creator. And our sages wrote that despite their desire to reach Judah as quickly as possible, she taught her that it is forbidden to walk on the Sabbath more than two thousand cubits beyond the last inhabited settlement. To this Ruth replied, "Where you go, I will go."

Naomi also taught her the code of Torah morality, including the prohibition of *yichud* (יִחוּד), seclusion with men. And this Ruth accepted: "Where you lodge, I will lodge."

According to our sages, when Naomi said to her: "We are commanded to fulfill six-hundred and thirteen precepts," Ruth replied: "Your people are my people."

"We are forbidden to worship idols."

"Your God is my God."

"My daughter, a Jew does not reside in a house that lacks a *mezuzah*."

"Where you lodge, I will lodge."

"Jewish maidens do not frequent pagan circuses and theaters."

"Where you go, I will go."

Ruth understood Naomi's hesitation to take her to Judah; she feared that no Jew would marry a Moabite woman since the prohibition against marrying Moabites was generally thought to extend also to women. Her answer was: "I will cleave to you and from your deeds learn how to cleave to God."

1:17   בַּאֲשֶׁר תָּמוּתִי אָמוּת וְשָׁם אֶקָּבֵר כֹּה יַעֲשֶׂה יְהֹוָה לִי וְכֹה יוֹסִיף כִּי הַמָּוֶת יַפְרִיד בֵּינִי וּבֵינֵךְ:

"Where you die, I will die; and there I will be buried. Thus may God do to me, and more, for death will separate me from you."

"I cannot bear to be without you. The moment you die, I will die. And may God deal severely with me if I permit anything but death to separate me from you."

Realizing that it was unlikely that any man in Judah would marry her, Ruth was prepared to live and die alone with Naomi, and be buried next to her rather than next to a husband.

"Death will separate me from you," she insisted, "but not my place of burial." Since, however, it was not within her power to determine when and where she would die and be buried, Ruth prayed that God grant that she remain free of sin and thus worthy of dying in the same place as Naomi, and hence be buried next to her.

Moreover, she prayed that her death and burial be in the Holy Land, for according to our sages, one who dies there is like a baby in his mother's arms, whereas one who dies elsewhere is like a baby in the arms of a stepmother. And one who is buried in the Holy Land is considered as if buried beneath the altar of the Holy Temple.

Then, realizing that she had spoken of Naomi's death before her own ("Where you die, I will die"), Ruth quickly corrected herself by adding, "Thus may God do to me . . . for death will separate me from you," mentioning her own death first.

According to the Midrash, Naomi had warned Ruth that one who accepts the Torah is liable for transgressions and subject to the four types of capital punishment. And Ruth replied: "In whatever way you die, I will die," expressing her acceptance of the Torah along with its specific punishments.

Then she added "may God do to me"—a prayer that she die a natural death rather than incur the death penalty for her sins.

According to our sages, "for death will separate me from you" also alludes to the teaching Ruth absorbed from her mother-in-law regarding life's purpose in this world: to fulfill as many *mitzvoth* as possible and accumulate good deeds for which one is rewarded in the World to Come. [She would strive for this by becoming a Jew and cleaving to Naomi.] In the hereafter, on the other hand, they will be "separate." For the souls of the righteous are uniquely rewarded in the World to Come, "each occupying a different abode" (Talmud).

The contrary is true of the gentiles who worship idols, whom death does not set apart. [Since they do not acknowledge the one true God, the source of all distinctions and differences in the world, the difference between living and non-living is denied]. "In life they are all as dead, and in death they are not separate" (Daily Prayer).

Accordingly, Ruth said: "Death will separate me from you," affirming her belief in life after death.

Moreover, אקבֹר כֹּה conveys her belief in the resurrection of the dead. The last four letters spell ברכה, blessing, which is an allusion to resurrection. Thus it is written, "For there has the Lord commanded the blessing (ברכה)—eternal life" (Psalms 133:3).

Ruth said, "Thus may God do to me." She prayed that the blessing Naomi had given her daughters-in-law ("May the Lord deal kindly . . ."—v. 8) should be fulfilled through her alone, now that Orpah returned to her gods. And more—may He add to this blessing ("find rest . . . in the house of her husband"—v. 9) so that from her marriage will come forth the royal dynasty.

1:18 וַתֵּרֶא כִּי־מִתְאַמֶּצֶת הִיא לָלֶכֶת אִתָּהּ וַתֶּחְדַּל לְדַבֵּר אֵלֶיהָ:

When she saw that she strove to go with her, she ceased speaking to her.

Naomi saw that the more she tried to dissuade Ruth from converting, the more resolute Ruth became. When she first said "Go, return" (v. 8), Ruth had replied, "With you we shall return to your people" (v. 10). And then instead of yielding to Naomi's persistent urging to the contrary, Ruth declared: "Where you go, I will go . . . where you die, I will die" (vs. 16, 17). Her words had the opposite effect she intended, and so Naomi ceased speaking.

In accordance with the teaching of our sages that a would-be convert is rejected with the left hand and befriended with the right, Naomi had tried to deter Ruth by instructing her in the penalties incurred for transgression of Torah precepts; and when Ruth embraced the Torah way nonetheless, she encouraged her by speaking of the reward of the righteous in the World to Come. Then "she ceased speaking to her," lest this would-be convert should be [encouraged or] discouraged excessively.

A further reason was that Naomi "saw" Ruth was trying to gain strength and ease her isolation by cleaving to her.

Another interpretation sees Ruth, not Naomi, as the subject of the verse. When Ruth saw that Naomi was determined to thrust her away, and fearing that she might be swayed, she stopped talking and began to walk alone toward Judah.

Ruth's perseverence is without parallel. Nowhere else does the Scripture use the term מתאמצת, for no other proselyte ever "strove" so tenaciously to cling to the *Shechinah* (Divine Presence).

Resh Lakish, then leader of a robber band, once leaped across the Jordan River in a single bound. When, however, Rabbi Yochanan subsequently persuaded him to dedicate his energies to Torah learning, he lost his strength and was unable to leap back (Baba Metzia 84a). Similarly, when Ruth accepted the yoke of the Torah, she became weak and had to exert herself ("she strove") to walk.

Moreover, this indicates that since Ruth was on the way to join a strange people, she had to struggle to keep pace with Naomi, who was returning home, even if laden with misfortune.

In return for her efforts, God strengthened Ruth as He strengthened all those who struggle to be righteous, as it is written: "He that has pure hands grows stronger and stronger" (Job 17:9).

1:19 וַתֵּלַכְנָה שְׁתֵּיהֶם עַד־בּוֹאָנָה בֵּית לָחֶם וַיְהִי כְּבוֹאָנָה בֵּית לֶחֶם וַתֵּהֹם כָּל־הָעִיר עֲלֵיהֶן וַתֹּאמַרְנָה הֲזֹאת נָעֳמִי׃

The two of them went until they came to Bethlehem. And it came to pass as they came to Bethlehem that the whole city was astir over them. And they said, "Is this Naomi?"

Along the dangerous roads of Moab, where Orpah encountered a hundred Philistines on her way home and may have been raped, "the two of them" walked alone. They did not even wait for a caravan.

For protection, they disguised themselves as men, hence the masculine ending of the word שְׁתֵּיהֶם, instead of שְׁתֵּיהֶן. And miraculously, they encountered no one until they reached Bethlehem.

They were now "the two of them"—equal in purpose and determination. Although Ruth was moving farther and farther away from her birthplace and approaching a strange land where she knew people would look strangely at her, she walked with the same eagerness as Naomi, who was returning home.

Our sages infer from here how greatly God cherishes the proselyte. Once Ruth had resolved to convert, the scripture holds her to be equal to the righteous and noble Naomi.

Since Elimelech and Naomi and their two sons had been prominent citizens of Bethlehem, all the people approached to greet her. To their amazement, the same Naomi who had always gone out attended by a retinue of servants dressed in finery, was now returning home alone and in rags, her once radiant face sallow and haggard. It caused a great commotion, and the people kept saying to one another in wonder, "Could this be Naomi?"

Ruth 1

The tragic figure of Naomi evoking the wonder of Bethlehem's citizens is also symbolic of the fallen Jerusalem evoking the wonder of the nations. "Is this the city that was called the perfection of beauty," they ask, "the joy of the whole earth?" (Lamentations 2:15).

Bethlehem was astir "over them," not merely over Naomi, for Ruth's striking beauty, contrasting sharply with Naomi's terrible appearance, intensified their amazement. Accordingly, וַתֹּאמַרְנָה—the feminine form—conveys that the women drew closer to assure themselves that they had identified Naomi correctly. Perhaps not the broken old woman, but the beautiful young one beside her, was really Naomi.

"Is this Naomi?" The question may have been addressed to Ruth. Yet they did not ask "Is this your mother-in-law?" since they did not know Ruth, or else because they did not want to embarrass Naomi by reminding her that her son had married a Moabite.

By coming out to greet Naomi, the Bethlehemites fulfilled the obligation of a society to share in the sorrow of the individual. At the same time, from Naomi's present condition they drew the proper lesson for themselves and repented of their own misdeeds.

Said R. Yitzchak: Read not הזאת נעמי ("Is this Naomi?") but חזאת נעמי (as in חזות, seeing)—i.e., "have you seen Naomi?" "Look at what happened to Naomi for leaving the Holy Land!" they said to one another. But then they added: "If this is Naomi—the one whose deeds were pleasing to God and to men—if it be that same Naomi who is reduced to such straits, then surely God will deal kindly with her now. For His mercies are not exhausted (Lamentations 3:22)."

According to the Jerusalem Talmud, the people had gathered then for the funeral of the wife of Boaz, who died that day. This is hinted at by the word *vay'ehi*, "it came to pass," which expresses woe (see verse 1). This explains how they all happened to be on hand when Ruth and Naomi arrived.

When the huge crowd following the bier saw these two unattended women coming, they approached them in greeting.

"One left, the other came," comments the Talmud. As soon as Boaz lost his first wife, God brought him Ruth.

Ruth's arrival in Bethlehem is a portent that Esau will rule over Jacob until the Messiah comes from Bethlehem. For as the prophet says: "And you, Bethlehem, Ephrata, youngest to be among the thousands of Judah, out of you shall come forth for Me that is to be the ruler in Israel" (Mica 5:1).

Thus, the first letters of ותלכנה ש׳תיהם ע׳ד, when spelled backwards, read עשו (Esau), and בואנה is an anagram of נבואה (prophecy). This implies that the power of Esau will last until the Messianic prophecy comes true.

1:20 וַתֹּאמֶר אֲלֵיהֶן אַל־תִּקְרֶאנָה לִי נָעֳמִי קְרֶאןָ לִי מָרָא כִּי־הֵמַר שַׁדַּי לִי מְאֹד׃

She said to them, "Call me not Naomi (pleasant), call me Mara (bitter); for the Almighty has dealt very bitterly with me."

Although surrounded by the entire population of Bethlehem, Naomi modestly addressed herself only to the women; hence "to them" in the feminine form (אליהן).

"Call me not Naomi, the pleasant one," she said, "but Mara, the bitter one." And to accent the great bitterness with which "the Almighty has dealt with me," the word *mara* ends in an unexpected *aleph* (א) rather than the letter *heh* (ה). Thus we find, similarly, "He left in a great wrath (חמא)" (Daniel 11:44)—חמא for emphasis, instead of the expected חמה.

In this regard, the numerical values of the א (= 1) and the ה (= 5) are significant. Of the five souls that left the land of Israel—Naomi, Elimelech, Machlon and Kilyon, and an unborn child—only one returned.

That she had been pregnant at the time is conveyed by "I went out full (מלאה)" (v. 21), as in, "the bones [that grow] in a full (מלאה) womb" (Ecclesiastes 11:5).

Therefore Naomi called herself Mara, Aramaic for "hoe," as if to say, "I have dug graves for my husband and children."

God had dealt "bitterly" with her by striking down her husband; "very" bitterly by striking down her two sons.

Naomi is also alluding to the fact that at the same time this was happening in Moab, her daughter, brothers, and sisters had died of the pestilence in the land of Israel.

Naomi observed that the people were not so much sorrowing over her tragic situation as bemoaning her fall from good fortune and previous situation in life. So she said: "So great is my suffering that you could well call me Mara even if I had not been Naomi, but one of the common people. As it is, however, falling from a great height made my suffering all the more bitter."

Naomi was like that recalcitrant cow put up for sale in the marketplace, whose owner praised her diligence at plowing and making beautiful furrows.

"If so," queried a prospective buyer, "why does she show all those tell-tale signs of having been beaten!"

Similarly, when Naomi, who had been famous for her good deeds, saw that the Bethlehemites around her were appalled to see a righteous woman in such straits, she said to them, "Call me not Naomi, she whose deeds are pleasing, but Mara, she whose deeds are bitter. Had I been truly righteous, God would not have dealt so bitterly with me."

1:21 אֲנִי מְלֵאָה הָלַכְתִּי וְרֵיקָם הֱשִׁיבַנִי יְהוָה לָמָּה תִקְרֶאנָה לִי נָעֳמִי וַיהוָה עָנָה בִי וְשַׁדַּי הֵרַע־לִי:

"I went out full, and empty has the Lord returned me. Why should you call me Naomi, when the Lord has testified against me and the Almighty has afflicted me?"

Since no human being ever feels he has enough material possessions, our sages deduce that she was actually saying: "When I left the land of Israel, I was pregnant ("full") and had sons and daughters, health and wealth."

Now the word ענה may connote affliction, and also mean "answered." Accordingly she was saying: "The Lord had then fulfilled all my wishes and the name Naomi fit me. But now that the Almighty has afflicted me and I have lost everything, why should you still call me Naomi?"

She was like that rich man who came on hard times, had to sell his house and all his possessions, and was left with only his horse and wagon. Then he was forced to sell these also, and from then on had to carry heavy loads on his back. An old acquaintance who remembered him from his days of wealth met him and asked, "Where is all the gold and silver you once had?"

"Gold and silver?" he replied. "Would that I had a horse and wagon!"

Similarly, Naomi said: "Why remind me of my glorious old days by calling me Naomi? Would that I had what even the lowliest human being has! But the Almighty has dealt bitterly with me."

She was now "empty" of family, health, and possessions, and the fact that she returned at all was only due to divine mercy. The attribute of mercy is denoted by the Tetragrammaton (י׳ה׳ו׳ה׳); hence "empty has the Lord (י־ה־ו־ה) returned me."

The people of Bethlehem knew Naomi to be righteous, and they ascribed her misfortunes to יסורים של אהבה, suffering that God visits upon the righteous in order to increase their reward. She however objected: "Why do you call me Naomi, she whose deeds are pleasing, when God is afflicting me for my sins?

"God is just, and He has punished me measure for measure. Because I went out full—I left the land of Israel during the famine, although I had food—God has returned me empty. Therefore do not call me Naomi as if my actions were pleasing."

Lest the people, however, object that it was her husband who sinned by fleeing from the responsibility of feeding the poor and hungry, Naomi added: "The Lord has testified against me." She too was guilty for failing to protest.

The term ענה can mean warned, testified, or humbled. "The Lord warned me to repent, but I paid no heed; whereupon He punished me, thereby testifying that I had sinned; and He humbled me." Similarly the prophet says, "The glory of Israel shall be humbled" (Hosea 5:5).

Naomi's punishment was inflicted not by the divine Attribute of Justice (*Elohim*), but by the Attribute of Mercy ("the Lord") operating on behalf of the poor. For as the Torah states: "If he [a poor man] calls out to Me, I will hear, for I am merciful" (Exodus 22:26).

The punishment for afflicting the poor is harsh and long-lasting. Naomi asked that she no longer be called Naomi, being convinced that her bitter condition would endure.

Although Naomi said, "the Almighty has afflicted me," she realized that what she called affliction was only to "me," that is, according to her human perception. But in truth, everything God does is good. Thus our sages teach: "In this world, for happy events we recite the blessing ברוך הטוב והמטיב, "Exalted is He Who is good and does good," and on sad occasions we recite, ברוך דין אמת, "Blessed is the True Judge." In the future, however, we will recite only "Exalted is He Who is good and does good," for we will realize that our suffering was the source of our good fortune, as it is written: "I will rejoice over them to do good for them, and I will plant them in this land in truth with My whole heart and with My whole soul" (Jeremiah 32:41).

1:22 וַתָּשָׁב נָעֳמִי וְרוּת הַמּוֹאֲבִיָּה כַלָּתָהּ עִמָּהּ הַשָּׁבָה מִשְּׂדֵי מוֹאָב וְהֵמָּה בָּאוּ בֵּית לֶחֶם בִּתְחִלַּת קְצִיר שְׂעֹרִים:

Thus Naomi returned, and with her Ruth the Moabite, her daughter-in-law, who returned from the Fields of Moab. They came [to] Bethlehem at the beginning of the barley harvest.

The narrative of Naomi's return, interrupted to record her acceptance of God's judgment, is now resumed. Scripture repeats that "Naomi returned." For as we find in Genesis, when the narrative about Joseph is resumed, the scripture repeats that "Joseph was taken down to Egypt" (Genesis 39:1), making explicit the link between the earlier events affecting him and those that were to follow.

Our sages teach that she "returned" in more ways than one. She "returned" to God; she repented. It is stressed once more that she came "to Bethlehem," the very place she had left to escape the poor and hungry. She willingly accepted the pain of facing her old acquaintances for the sake of living in the Holy Land, thus atoning for having left the land.

She also returned to her good deeds. The poor had called her Naomi (the pleasant) because she collected money for them and dispensed comfort with a pleasant word. No one had taken her place while she was gone, and now she resumed her work of charity assisted by Ruth, who cleaved to her in order to learn the ways of righteousness.

On account of Ruth, who stayed "with her" and brought her happiness, Naomi began to rise out of the depths of misery she had reached in Moab, and to return to her former self. Therefore she continues to be called Naomi, even though she had asked to be called Mara (the bitter).

Evidently Naomi also returned to her original level of righteousness, since she merited to bring back from Moab the mother of royalty.

Although Ruth was now fully a Jewess, she is still called "the Moabite," reflecting the fact that her Moabite origin enabled her to guide Naomi safely out of Moab.

The scripture provides the extra emphasis that "Ruth ... returned from the Fields of Moab," calling attention to Ruth's greatness. She had separated herself from the stinginess and depravity of Moab to cleave to the Jewish people, even though it meant leaving the life of a royal princess to glean in the fields. Hence the import of "they came . . . at the beginning of the barley harvest."

When God directed Abraham to the land of Israel, He said לֶךְ לְךָ, literally, "Go to yourself," for Abraham's soul was rooted in the holiness of that land. Ruth's soul likewise stemmed from the holiness of the land of Israel, but had been diverted into the impurity of Moab. Now it returned to its source.

So strong was the pull to return to her source, that Ruth came to the Holy Land even though her Moabite origin virtually precluded the possibility of marrying there.

Our sages comment: "It was she who returned from the Fields of Moab." God was waiting for two "pearls" to come from Moab and Ammon, and for their sake He forbade Israel to war with those nations. It now became apparent that Ruth was the long-awaited pearl from Moab.

She was also the first to "return from the Fields of Moab," in that she was the first Moabite to convert. And through her the forgotten law of "a Moabite, not a Moabitess" was clarified.

Previously it says (v. 19), "*until* they came [to] Bethlehem"; that is, Naomi and Ruth had then arrived at the outskirts of the city. Now they "came to Bethlehem." They entered the city proper.

They arrived "at the beginning of the barley harvest," that is, when the first-yield measure (*omer*, עֹמֶר) of barley is brought to the cohen-priest, in fulfillment of "You shall bring an *omer* of the first of your harvest to the priest. . . . And bread of parched corn and green ears you shall not eat until this self-same day, until you have brought the offering. . . ." (Leviticus 23:10-14). Thus the *omer* offering is called "the beginning of the barley harvest." Thereafter the new grain may be harvested and eaten.

In their eagerness to come to the land of Israel, Naomi and Ruth did not wait until the wheat season, but came at the harvest of barley, the first grain to ripen. And they arrived in time to participate in the *omer* offering—a demonstration of the principle that "one *mitzvah* brings in its wake another *mitzvah*."

To them, therefore, applies: "You mighty of strength, who fulfill His word, to harken to His word" (Psalms 103:20). Because they exerted themselves to fulfill one *mitzvah* ("His word"), they also merited to fulfill a second one.

Ruth 1

The pause mark (תפחא) over the word בתחלת ("at the beginning") is significant, indicating that it was a special beginning, namely, the first harvest after many years of famine.

According to Targum Yonathan, they came on the day before Passover, the beginning of the barley season, when the *omer* is harvested. This explains why Boaz did not come out to greet them. As the head of the clan, he was occupied with the Passover lamb offering and the baking of *matzoth*.

Thus begins the account of how it came to pass that Ruth married Boaz. Since "they came to Bethlehem at the beginning of the barley harvest," Ruth went to pick in the fields. . . .

RUTH 2

2:1 וּלְנָעֳמִי מידע (מוֹדַע קרי) לְאִישָׁהּ אִישׁ גִּבּוֹר חַיִל מִמִּשְׁפַּחַת אֱלִימֶלֶךְ וּשְׁמוֹ בֹּעַז:

Now Naomi had a kinsman of her husband, a mighty man of valor of the family of Elimelech. His name was Boaz.

The scripture now begins to reveal how, through Naomi's efforts, Ruth married Boaz. Thus came true Ruth's words, "With [i.e., through] you we shall return to your people" (v. 1:10).

His name describes his character. *Boaz* (בּוֹ־עַז)—in him there is strength. He was "a mighty man of valor (חַיִל)" who vanquished and abandoned his evil inclination, בֹּעַז being an anagram of עָזַב, abandoned; and he was mighty in Torah wisdom, which is acquired through the forty-eight (numerical value of חַיִל) virtues. To him thus applies, "A wise man is strong (*baoz*, בָּעוֹז); a man of knowledge increases strength" (Proverbs 24:5).

Furthermore, he is identified as Ibetzan, one of the chieftain-judges who protected Israel from her enemies (Judges 12:8). And his prayer saved Israel from the famine.

He was a descendant of Judah and bore within him the seeds of the royal dynasty.

The term מוֹדַע evidently means "kinsman," for as Boaz was later to say to Ruth: "There is also a redeemer closer than I" (v. 3:12). Thus, although Naomi had this wealthy kinsman of noble lineage who would have readily helped her, she preferred to receive her sustenance through *leket*, the gleaning in the field which the Torah awards the poor. By refusing to accept gifts from a relative, she was true to the teaching that "one who hates gifts shall live" (Proverbs 15:27).

She did, however, rely on her well-known kinship to the eminent Boaz to protect her daughter-in-law from being molested while picking in the fields.

Naomi "had a kinsman of her husband"; they were, however, also related from her side of the family. For as she was to say later: "The man is related to *us*" (v. 20)—both she and Elimelech were related to Boaz.

Thus the Talmud records the tradition that the father of Boaz, Salmon (Ruth 4:21); Elimelech, Plony Almony (4:1), and Naomi's father were all sons of Nachshon son of Aminadav, prince of the tribe of Judah. (An amended text there reads: Elimelech, Salmon, Boaz, and Naomi's father were all the sons of Nachshon son of Aminadav.)

This dual kinship is here alluded to in the word מוֹדָע ("kinsman") appearing between ולנעמי ("Naomi") and לאשה ("of her husband"). So the verse can be read "Naomi had a kinsman," or else "a kinsman of her husband."

The scripture nonetheless calls Boaz "a kinsman of her husband" because once a woman leaves her father's house for that of her husband, she is closer to her husband than to her father. However, Naomi's name appears first to reflect her personal stature.

Since Boaz has been identified as a kinsman of her husband, the phrase "of the family of Elimelech" would seem to be superfluous. But this accents that even among the distinguished family of Elimelech, Boaz stood out as "a mighty man of valor."

Elimelech is mentioned also for another reason—to contrast him with Boaz. Both were righteous men and both were descendants of Nachshon son of Aminadav, of Peretz and Judah, but neither personal worth nor ancestral merit were of any help to him when he abandoned the land of Israel.

Elimelech—אלי־מלך, "let kingship come to me"—foresaw that the monarchy would come through Moab, and went there to seek it. But his ambition was not fulfilled. Boaz on the other hand made no effort in this direction, indeed, was even willing to give away the kingship by offering another the opportunity of wedding Ruth. So God awarded him the privilege of being the forefather of David.

The word מוֹדָע, "kinsman," is spelled with the letter *yud* (י, numerically equivalent to 10), rather than with the expected *vav* (ו, מודע) to hint to the ten years that Naomi lived in Moab (v. 1:4). For during this time Boaz had repeatedly sent her messages urging her to return to the land of Israel and fulfill the commandment of aiding the poor, which is mentioned ten times in the Torah.

The letter *yud* also alludes to the ten generations from Abraham to Boaz. David had to be the fourteenth generation, so that Solomon [whose reign climaxed Israel's splendor as the bearer of God's glory on earth] would be the fifteenth generation, corresponding to the full moon on the fifteenth day of the lunar month. Had Salmon's brother Tov agreed to wed Ruth, the kingship of David would have had to wait an additional generation.

The unusual spelling of מידע also conveys that Boaz did not behave like a true kinsman. He knew that Naomi and Ruth had returned to Bethlehem in pitiful condition; for as he later said to Ruth, "It has been fully related to me all that you have done for your mother-in-law" (v. 11). Yet he offered them no immediate help, although they were so poor that Ruth was forced to go pick in the fields and, when that was not enough to sustain them, Naomi was forced to sell her field, as it is written: "The portion of field that was our brother Elimelech's has Naomi sold" (v. 4:3).

Or else, Boaz apparently estranged himself in order to test Ruth. How she reacted to her difficult circumstances would disclose whether she was worthy of entering his house.

Another interpretation is that Boaz did not come out to greet Naomi and Ruth upon their arrival in Bethlehem because he was in mourning for his wife, who had died that very day. It is revealing in this regard that when, after the week of mourning, he went out to his fields, the fieldhands did not greet him until he greeted them. This accords with the halacha that one who is in mourning greets others; others do not greet him first.

When he then saw Ruth gleaning there, he understood that Naomi did not want to accept help from her relatives. Out of respect for her wishes, he refrained from offering her gifts [and helped instead through his benevolent treatment of Ruth while she gleaned in his field.]

Moreover, he knew that they owned fields and other possessions. For as he was to say later (v. 4:9), "I have purchased all that is Elimelech's and all that is Kilyon's and Machlon's from the hand of Naomi." It also stands to reason that [when they left Bethlehem for Moab] Elimelech and Naomi had not sold any part of their fields, since Torah law forbids selling a field and hoarding the purchase money.

2:2 וַתֹּאמֶר רוּת הַמּוֹאֲבִיָּה אֶל־נָעֳמִי אֵלְכָה־נָּא הַשָּׂדֶה וַאֲלַקֳטָה בַשִׁבֳּלִים אַחַר אֲשֶׁר אֶמְצָא־חֵן בְּעֵינָיו וַתֹּאמֶר לָהּ לְכִי בִתִּי׃

Ruth the Moabite said to Naomi: "I will go now to the field

and glean among the ears of grain, behind one in whose eyes I shall find favor."

She said to her, "Go, my daughter."

The scripture now narrates how it came to pass that Boaz encountered Ruth.

As soon as they arrived in Bethlehem, Ruth set out to provide for herself in order not to burden Naomi. Moreover, she undertook to support her mother-in-law as well—a great kindness which set her apart from the Moabite people, who had not greeted Israel with bread and water.

The daughter of the king of Moab proposed to pick in the fields with the paupers. "I will go"—gladly—"for the ears of grain I will pick in the fields of Israel are more precious to me than the diamonds in my father's palace."

Ruth tactfully spared Naomi's feelings. Claiming that she, a stranger from Moab, could glean without embarrassment, she insisted that Naomi stay home while she went to the fields alone. "I will go"—I and not you.

Lest, however, visitors arrive in the meantime to see Naomi's daughter-in-law leave for the fields, Ruth left "now"—early in the morning, tired though she was from the long journey.

Although their destitution made picking in the fields necessary for survival, Ruth honored her mother-in-law by asking permission before she went.

Her plan was to inspect "*the* field," that is, the field of Elimelech. On the way back, she would pick with the poor.

Or else, "the field" refers to the fields of Boaz, which would mean that he had welcomed them as soon as they had arrived.

Another interpretation is that since Ruth had no friend or relative in whose field she could pick, she would simply try whatever field she chanced upon. If the owner treated her kindly and generously, she would pick there; if not, she would go elsewhere, until she found a field whose owner looked upon her favorably.

(Evidently an ungenerous landowner could prevent the poor from taking what was rightfully theirs, or else the custom was not to let women pick without permission.)

She would select a field whose owner's eyes had "favor," that is, looked into the Torah rather than at women, and looked kindly upon the pickings of the poor. She would pick only behind a reaper who was righteous.

Some say that Ruth was ashamed to glean among the poor and preferred to earn her livelihood by working. She would look for a landowner interested in hiring her to work in his field. This is indicated by "in whose eyes I shall find favor." Merely to partake of what by Torah law she could pick freely, she had no need to find favor. When therefore Boaz's manservant later said (v. 7), "She came and has been on her feet ever since the morning," he was referring to her work as a hired field-hand.

She hinted that she would not be pursuing young men who might appeal to her, but would wait to find favor in the eyes of a righteous man.

Knowledgeable in the laws that Naomi had taught her regarding giving to the poor, she now assured Naomi that she would not avail herself of *peah*—picking in the corner of the field set aside for the poor (Leviticus 19:9)—because there she would be competing with other paupers. Nor would she take *shikechah*—ears that the reapers forgot to cut (Leviticus 23:22)—because it is difficult to ascertain which ears are truly forgotten. She would only gather the *leket* (לקט, hence ואלקטה)—ears that fell from the reaper's hands as he cut (ibid.). And, in observance of the halacha that more than two ears that fell together at a time are not *leket*, she would gather only ב' שבלים, lit. two ears.

Convinced that Ruth's behavior in the field would be in keeping with modesty, good manners, and the halacha, Naomi consented. And because Ruth felt lonely and strange, she added a word of encouragement: "Do not think of yourself as the Moabite, but as my daughter. I allow you to go only because necessity forces me to; for I cherish and esteem you like a daughter."

The expression "my daughter" does not necessarily indicate that Ruth was a young girl. In fact, our sages say she was forty years of age at the time.

The extreme poverty that forced Ruth to pick in the fields like any pauper was no coincidence, but was a foreshadowing of that "poor man, riding on a donkey" (Zechariah 9:9) who would descend from her—the Messiah.

Ruth 2

2:3 וַתֵּלֶךְ וַתָּבוֹא וַתְּלַקֵּט בַּשָּׂדֶה אַחֲרֵי הַקֹּצְרִים וַיִּקֶר מִקְרֶהָ חֶלְקַת הַשָּׂדֶה לְבֹעַז אֲשֶׁר מִמִּשְׁפַּחַת אֱלִימֶלֶךְ:

She went; she came and gleaned in the field behind the reapers; and it was her lot to happen upon the portion of field belonging to Boaz, who was of the family of Elimelech.

Ruth "went" from her mother-in-law's house and "came" to the field of Elimelech, which was now leased and later (v. 4:9) sold to Boaz because he was "of the family of Elimelech."

Or else, she "went" looking for the field of Elimelech, but "came" upon the adjacent field of his kinsman Boaz.

According to another interpretation, Ruth set out for the field of Boaz, who had welcomed them upon their arrival, and God led her directly there.

To familiarize herself with the new place, Ruth "went" and "came" many times. And she marked the road so that she would not lose her way and have to ask directions of passers-by, who might engage her in lengthy conversations for the wrong reasons.

Rabbi Eleazar said: She came and went until she found righteous people to go with.

Eager to be self-supporting rather than dependent on charity, she came and went the entire harvest season, toiling tirelessly six days a week, as hinted by the extra letter *vav* (ו) in ותבוא, "she came" (ו is numerically equivalent to 6). She would go to the field, pick all she could carry, take it home, and return to pick more. To avoid carrying her heavy load a long distance, she would first go to the end of the field ("she went") and then pick on her way back ("she came").

According to another interpretation, Ruth "went" and "came" from one field to another until she happened upon the field of Boaz, where she remained. For there, her heart told her, lay her destiny.

Even after coming to the field of Boaz, she inspected other fields to ascertain where the people were the most worthy. She found no place to compare with the field of Boaz, where everyone was righteous.

The Talmud says that it was because Boaz's reapers were righteous that God arranged for Ruth to come to his field; so beautiful was she, that anyone of lesser virtue came to sinful thought at the sight of her.

Boaz welcomed Ruth and instructed his reapers deliberately to "forget" many sheaves—even forget "for her from the heaps" (v. 16). So it was that after going ("she went") through the field once, on her way back ("she came"), she found still more to pick.

God directed Ruth to the field of Boaz, where she was able to pick enough to sustain both herself and Naomi, and was treated with dignity and respect. This was only the beginning of His kindness to her, for God does not withhold good from those who walk in perfect faith. He now began to uplift Ruth and Naomi from poverty and hunger to kingship.

This is a lesson to all later generations, to place their trust in God in times of distress.

2:4 וְהִנֵּה־בֹעַז בָּא מִבֵּית לֶחֶם וַיֹּאמֶר לַקּוֹצְרִים יְהֹוָה עִמָּכֶם וַיֹּאמְרוּ לוֹ יְבָרֶכְךָ יְהֹוָה:

Behold! Boaz came from Bethlehem. He said to the reapers, "The Lord be with you." And they said to him, "May the Lord bless you."

Boaz would not usually come out to the field. But on that day, "Behold!"—suddenly, unexpectedly, he came.

Another sudden, unexpected visit is recorded in the Talmud. A poor, hungry man once asked Rava for a meal of fattened chicken and old wine, and just then Rava's sister, whom he had not seen for years, appeared unexpectedly, bringing with her a gift of fattened chicken and old wine. Realizing that divine providence had arranged the visit so that the pauper would be fed according to his needs, Rava invited him to eat.

Similarly, when Boaz unexpectedly visited his field and saw Ruth, he understood that divine providence had arranged that he had come for her benefit. As soon as he had exchanged greetings with his workers, he therefore immediately inquired, "To whom is this young woman?" (v. 5).

It is a measure of his humility that the eminent Boaz greeted his reapers even before they greeted him.

He blessed them that God should protect them from sunstroke, since the sun's rays are particularly strong during the harvest season. Thus the Shunamite woman's son suffered sunstroke in the field during the harvest (2 Kings 4).

At the splendid sight of his grain-filled field and his workers busily harvesting, Boaz exclaimed: "God be in your thoughts always! Do not allow material abundance to make you forget Him. Consider that you are working now so that you can be free for Torah study the rest of the year.

"Remember God Who commanded us to observe the laws connected with the harvest—*peah*, *leket*, and *shikechah*. Welcome the poor graciously and treat them kindly, lest God depart from your midst."

They replied: "Your good intentions will lead to blessings and abundance.

"We have indeed fulfilled the *mitzvoth* of the harvest, for which God will bless you (יברכך ה')." Thus our sages teach: "Separate a tenth-part tithe (עַשֵׂר תְּעַשֵׂר, Deuteronomy 14:22)—separate the tithe (עַשֵׂר) that you may become rich (תִּתְעַשֵׁר)."

And the reapers blessed Boaz for his generosity to the poor, as it is written, "He who is generous of eye shall be blessed" (Proverbs 22:9).

According to a different interpretation, Boaz had just arisen from the seven days of mourning for his wife. In keeping with the halacha that the mourner does not exchange greetings with others, Boaz now greeted his fellow man for the first time since the death of his wife, and the reapers returned his greeting.

They blessed him with the name "the Lord" (the Tetragrammaton), which denotes the divine attribute of mercy. Since divine justice, which had just struck him, continues to attend the mourner for some time after the tragedy, they prayed that God deal with him henceforth only through the attribute of mercy.

Thus the Talmud (Moed Koton 27b) writes: "The entire first three days, the mourner should imagine a sword poised between his shoulders; from the third day until the seventh, as if it were standing drawn against him in a corner; from the seventh to the thirtieth day, as receding."

A man without a wife, say our sages, is without blessing. So the reapers said, "May the Lord bless you," meaning, "God send you a suitable wife." They hinted that Ruth was the woman who would restore him to a blessed state.

According to our sages, Boaz was now coming from the House of Study (*Beit Midrash*), filled with the joy of Torah study. This is conveyed by the joyful expression "behold." There, he and his court had just enacted the decree that people use the Holy Name (Tetragrammaton) in greeting one another, so that the name of God would always be on their lips. In a generation when the people judged their judges, the court deemed it necessary to implant the belief in divine providence.

According to the Talmud (Makoth 23b), this was one of the decrees by an earthly court which was ratified by the heavenly Tribunal. Thus we find the angel greeting Gideon: "The Lord be with you, mighty man of valor" (Judges 6:12).

(This accords with the view that Boaz lived during the time of Barak and Deborah, who preceded Gideon [see v. 1:1]. According to the opinion that Boaz is the judge Ibetzan, who came after Gideon, the angel had set the precedent, and Boaz and his court put it into practice.)

Coming now from the *Beit Midrash* where the decree had just been instituted, Boaz was the first to implement it by greeting his reapers with "The Lord be with you"; and they replied in kind.

Indeed, they blessed him for the decree, making it clear they understood that its purpose was to implant the belief that God affects the affairs of this world. Blessing and abundance would result, as it is written: "Every place where My name is mentioned I will come to you and bless you" (Exodus 20:21).

Blessing follows whenever God's name is mentioned in connection with the performance of a *mitzvah*. And since inclusion of God's name in greeting was now made a *mitzvah* by answering as they did, they were in effect blessing him with abundance.

Our sages conclude that [the converse is also true]. If God's name is mentioned in vain, poverty follows.

The harvesters returned Boaz's greeting in two brief words—יברכך ה'—because an employee should refrain from conversation during work hours. Thus the Talmud relates that when Abba Chilkiyah would work for an employer, he did not even return the greeting of the sages.

Similarly, when one is preoccupied with the performance of any *mitzvah*, such as teaching Torah to children, or making burial arrangements, he should be brief in replying to others.

Moreover, the reaper's brief blessing conveys that one should preferably use a form of blessing that explicitly appears in the scripture. Their blessing, appropriate for the season, is contained in, "Blessed are you in the city; blessed are you in the field" (Deuteronomy 28:3).

Boaz began his greeting with God's name and the reapers ended theirs with it, in order to begin and end with the divine name. This is the source of the custom that people greet one another with "*Shalom*

Ruth 2

Aleichem" and reply with "*Aleichem Shalom*" [so as to begin and end with *Shalom*, peace, which is also one of God's names].

Another interpretation is that when Boaz saw a beautiful woman in the field, he feared that the *Shechinah* had left them, for God's presence cannot dwell where there is impropriety. He therefore inquired: "Is God with you?"

2:5 וַיֹּאמֶר בֹּעַז לְנַעֲרוֹ הַנִּצָּב עַל־הַקּוֹצְרִים לְמִי הַנַּעֲרָה הַזֹּאת:

Boaz said to his servant who stood over the reapers: "To whom is this young woman?"

When he saw a woman picking in the field, Boaz assumed that one of the reapers had brought her. "To whom is this young woman?" he asked.

Or else, when he noticed that she was obviously of a different people, he reprimanded his overseer for allowing her to enter.

According to a different interpretation, Boaz inquired about her in response to the reapers' hint that this virtuous and modest woman would make him a suitable wife.

He perceived that she was no ordinary pauper, but a person of breeding and distinction. In contrast to the common pauper who greedily seizes whatever comes his way, she ate with restraint even after going hungry for a long time; moreover, she was embarrassed to accept charity. He therefore expressed his surprise that this fine woman was not married.

Our sages note that he saw in her signs of wisdom and modesty. In observance of the halacha, she picked two ears of corn but not three, and was careful to take only sheaves that were definitely abandoned. She picked the uncut ears while standing and the already plucked while sitting; she did not bend over. She went "behind the reapers" (v. 3) rather than among or beside them. And upon seeing Boaz, she modestly turned away.

"All the other women flirt with the reapers," remarked Boaz, "and this one keeps to herself; all the other women pick among the sheaves, and this one picks only what is abandoned" (*Midrash*).

The *Zohar* states that this judge of Israel saw that she possessed humility, divine insight (*ruach hakodesh*, רוח הקודש), and a "benevolent eye" which brought blessing to whatever she gazed upon.

He therefore asked, "To whom does she belong? For whom is she gathering?" Without asking directly, he would thus ascertain whether she was single or married.

2:6 וַיַּעַן הַנַּעַר הַנִּצָּב עַל־הַקּוֹצְרִים וַיֹּאמַר נַעֲרָה מוֹאֲבִיָּה הִיא הַשָּׁבָה עִם־נָעֳמִי מִשְּׂדֵי מוֹאָב:

The man who was standing over the reapers answered and said: "A Moabite young woman is she, who returned with Naomi from the Fields of Moab."

The overseer whom Boaz addressed was "standing over the reapers" in a high, prominent place so that his voice would carry far. Our sages point out that he was supervising forty-two harvesters. This is the maximum number of workers that one person can oversee, as we learn from Solomon, who appointed 3,600 to oversee 150,000 (2 Chronicles 2:1).

"The man answered" (*va'ya'an*, וַיַּעַן, of the root ענה). The word ענה can mean "answered" as well as "raised his voice." The overseer understood from Boaz's discreet inquiry that he might be interested in marrying Ruth, and in excited anger he raised his voice when replying. "She has just returned with Naomi from Moab and converted," he said.

According to this interpretation, he hinted that the marriage was unsuitable for several reasons. First, she was an extraordinarily beautiful "young woman" of forty, Boaz a very old man; and our sages oppose wedding young to old. Second, she was a Moabite.

The distinction in halacha of "a Moabite, not a Moabitess" was not yet well known, and the overseer was ignorant of it. Or else, even if he did know it, he still thought it improper for a man like Boaz to marry her. Indeed, even Plony Almony (v. 4:1) later refused to rely on this halachic distinction, and so should Boaz, who was a greater sage. Were there not enough Israelite girls, conceived and born in holiness, for him to wed?

Third, he implied that she converted only because she wanted to be "with Naomi." Fourth, she came from "the Fields of Moab" where the people were miserly and evil. And she may have been raped by them along the way.

Other commentaries explain that the overseer was in fact praising her to Boaz. This woman was young enough, he intimated, to bear him children and replace his sons who had all died (Talmud, Baba Bathra 91a). Moreover, being a Moabite woman, not a man, she was permitted to marry a Jew. Her conversion was purely for the sake of heaven, considering that she had abandoned the life of a princess to return with the destitute Naomi. And although she was born and bred in Moab, such was her purity of character that she lived in peace even with her mother-in-law.

Some early commentators perceive a difficulty here; for the verse says that she "returned from the Fields of Moab," yet she had never before been in Bethlehem. This suggests that she had gone back to Moab in order to convert others of her family, and not succeeding, returned.

2:7 וַתֹּאמֶר אֲלַקֳטָה־נָּא וְאָסַפְתִּי בָעֳמָרִים אַחֲרֵי הַקּוֹצְרִים וַתָּבוֹא וַתַּעֲמוֹד מֵאָז הַבֹּקֶר וְעַד־עַתָּה זֶה שִׁבְתָּהּ הַבַּיִת מְעָט:

"She said, 'Please let me glean and I will gather among the sheaves after the reapers.' So she came and has been on her feet ever since the morning until now, having sat in a house a little."

The overseer praised Ruth for her industriousness. After arriving in Bethlehem she had risen early in the morning and had been on her feet picking ever since, save for a brief rest at home. Because she was modest, went only where the reapers were righteous, and took no more than Torah law permits, the picking took her all day. By the words "having sat in the house a little," he intimated that at home, too, she tended diligently to the house, allowing herself little time to rest.

Perhaps he was also suggesting that Boaz hire her to work in his home.

According to a different interpretation, Ruth politely asked permission to glean the *leket*, even though the Torah rightfully assigns it to the poor. Furthermore, she asked that the *leket* she picked be in exchange for helping to gather the harvested sheaves. And because she then worked all day collecting sheaves, she managed to gather only a little for her mother-in-law.

Accordingly, "having sat in the house a little" suggests that Ruth was now resting briefly in the women's hut adjacent to the field, before returning to work.

From the extra letter *vav* (ו) in ותעמד ("was on her feet"), it is inferred that six hours (*vav* equals 6) had passed from the time she came in the morning until now, the hour of the midday meal.

Some however interpret his remarks as derogatory. The overseer was hinting that at first she had humbly asked permission to pick, but then remained to garner the entire day.

According to the Midrash, he said: "She has been with us a few days, but she is so modest and reserved that we know nothing about her, not even whether she is a widow."

Unknowingly, he prophesied ("having sat in a house a little") that she would remain in her own house for but a short time before marrying Boaz.

2:8 וַיֹּאמֶר בֹּעַז אֶל־רוּת הֲלֹא שָׁמַעַתְּ בִּתִּי אַל־תֵּלְכִי לִלְקֹט בְּשָׂדֶה אַחֵר וְגַם לֹא תַעֲבוּרִי מִזֶּה וְכֹה תִדְבָּקִין עִם־נַעֲרֹתָי:

Boaz said to Ruth: "Have you not heard, my daughter? Go not to glean in another field; neither pass from here, but stay here close to my girls."

Boaz had offered Ruth gifts of money and clothing, which she refused, insisting she would take only what God gave her. Whereupon Boaz urged her at least not to go to any other field—not even one owned by him—but to "stay here," where he would look after her and protect her.

"Have you not heard my overseer praise you?" he asked. "Why go to another field where you may be unwelcome or unappreciated? Stay where you are, on the women's side of my field."

Alternately: "Having heard me ask the overseer about you, perhaps you think I begrudge you your picking. On the contrary—I insist that you stay in my field and continue to pick behind the reapers, or, if you like, among the girls."

The expression הֲלוֹא, "have you not," contains an extra letter *vav* (ו, numerically equivalent to 6), to reflect the six times that the Torah speaks of the harvest (*katzir*, קָצִיר) and warns us to fulfill the harvest laws.

> *When you reap the harvest of your land, you shall not wholly reap the corner of your field, neither shall you gather the gleaning of your harvest (Leviticus 19:9). When you reap the harvest of your land, you shall not wholly reap the corner of your field, neither shall you gather the gleanings of your harvest; you shall leave them for the poor, and for the stranger: I am the Lord your God (Leviticus 23:22). That which grows of itself of your harvest you shall not reap, and the grapes of your undressed vine you shall not gather (Leviticus 25:5). When you reap your harvest in the field, and have forgotten a sheaf in the field, you shall not go back to fetch it; it shall be for the stranger, for the fatherless, and for the widow (Deuteronomy 24:19).*

In other words, Boaz said to her: "Have you not heard that six times the Torah declares that *peah, leket,* and *shikechah* belong to the poor?"

According to a different interpretation, Boaz asked Ruth whether she could hear him, for he spoke to her from a distance out of propriety. He also addressed her as "my daughter," to avoid any semblance of impure thought towards her. Hence his name Boaz—"in him there is strength."

His saintly conduct reflects the general practice among our sages to address every woman as "my daughter" as a ruse against the evil inclination.

The term שָׁמַעְתְּ means "understand" as well as "hear." And Boaz is thus also perceived as saying to Ruth: "Even if you understand the overseer's remark about you as being derogatory, nevertheless do not go to another field. If you did not so understand it, then surely you must not pass from here."

Or else: "Have you heard him criticize you for leaving your house too often ("having sat in the house a little"—v. 7)? Then to prevent any more evil talk, do not go to a different field, but stay here and pick with my girls."

Even according to the view that the overseer tried to discourage Boaz

Ruth 2

from marrying Ruth, by describing her as a poor Moabite who returned with Naomi, his remarks in fact highlighted her virtue. For he could find nothing to criticize about her character or conduct. On the contrary, Boaz foresaw that the royal dynasty would come from her, and he told her "not to glean in another field." He asked her not to "pass from here" even after she had picked her fill, thereby hinting that she would find her destiny with him.

2:9 עֵינַיִךְ בַּשָּׂדֶה אֲשֶׁר־יִקְצֹרוּן וְהָלַכְתְּ אַחֲרֵיהֶן הֲלוֹא צִוִּיתִי אֶת־הַנְּעָרִים לְבִלְתִּי נָגְעֵךְ וְצָמִת וְהָלַכְתְּ אֶל־הַכֵּלִים וְשָׁתִית מֵאֲשֶׁר יִשְׁאֲבוּן הַנְּעָרִים:

"Keep your eyes on the field that they will harvest, and walk after them. Have I not ordered my men not to touch you? When you grow thirsty, go to the vessels and drink from that which the men draw."

Boaz told Ruth to look the field over and pick wherever she liked; and he had instructed his men not to stop her. If the reapers finished harvesting this field, she was welcome to follow them to the next one. And he gave her permission not only to draw water, but even to drink of the water drawn by the men.

For her protection, he instructed her to walk "after them," that is, only behind the reapers, so that they would not gaze at her and come to sinful thoughts. In addition, he took the precaution of instructing his men not to touch her. When she became thirsty, she was not to accept water from any of the men, but to take only from the vessels, in order to keep herself above suspicion.

According to one interpretation, Ruth was not to follow the reapers but first to check the field; if they had already left it, she could then go in alone and pick. No one would harm her, since he had already forewarned his men.

Some commentators draw the opposite conclusion. She was not to go alone, but only "after *them*"—where there were many reapers.

However, the terms יִקְצֹרוּן, "they will harvest," and אַחֲרֵיהֶן, "after them," end with the letter *nun* (ן), the feminine form, implying that Boaz instructed her to follow his girls.

Some say that Boaz appointed her overseer—hence "keep your eyes on the field." Although she would have to mingle with the fieldhands in order to observe their work, this was not contrary to Torah law, for they were righteous men, and the halacha is that one woman may be alone with two or more righteous men. Nor would they harm her out of jealousy, for he had taken the precaution of warning them.

As overseer, she would not have to draw water for herself, but drink from what the men would draw for her.

Or else, Boaz asked her to keep her eyes on his field in order to increase its blessing, for he recognized that Ruth's "benevolent eye" brought blessing upon whatever fell under her gaze.

The expression צָמִתְ, "you will become thirsty," is missing a letter *yud* (י, equivalent to 10), to hint that ten wicked kings—including the infamous Manasseh (2 Kings 20,21)—would descend from her. Accordingly, he said to her later (v. 14), "and dip your morsel in the vinegar."

2:10 וַתִּפֹּל עַל־פָּנֶיהָ וַתִּשְׁתַּחוּ אָרְצָה וַתֹּאמֶר אֵלָיו מַדּוּעַ מָצָאתִי חֵן בְּעֵינֶיךָ לְהַכִּירֵנִי וְאָנֹכִי נָכְרִיָּה:

Then she fell on her face and bowed down to the ground, and said to him, "Why have I found favor in your eyes that you take note of me, though I am a foreigner?"

Ruth expressed her gratitude to Boaz by bowing down before him, and humbly asked why he had been so kind to her when she had done nothing to deserve it. "Why do you concern yourself about me—a foreigner— when there are so many poor unfortunate girls picking in the fields?"

Ruth's question was the proper response to Boaz's generosity, for it was possible that he had erred in identifying her and that his kindness had been meant for another.

From Boaz's response (v. 11), it is apparent that Ruth was asking whether his kindness to her was because "I am a foreigner," who, he feared, might return to her people if he did not encourage her.

According to a different interpretation, Ruth wished to know whether Boaz's kindness to her was simple generosity or a sign that he intended to marry her. "I do not know why I have found favor in your eyes," she said, "and it is unthinkable that you have intentions of marriage, for I belong to a people known for immorality and stinginess, a people who did not greet Israel with bread and water.

"Your forefather (Abraham) rejected Timnah, although she was a princess [and she therefore became a concubine to Elifaz, as it is written: '. . . the sister of Lotan was Timnah; and Timnah was a concubine of Elifaz son of Esau" (Genesis 36:12,22)]. Certainly you must despise me, a poor woman from a people whom God has forbidden to be accepted as converts."

At that moment, says the Midrash, the pertinent halacha had eluded Boaz. Whereupon a heavenly voice proclaimed: "'An Ammonite or a Moabite shall not enter the congregation of the Lord; even to the tenth generation shall none of them enter the congregation of the Lord forever' (Deuteronomy 23:4)—an Ammonite, not an Ammonitess; a Moabite, not a Moabitess."

Thus it was that that halacha was clarified on account of Ruth.

2:11 וַיַּעַן בֹּעַז וַיֹּאמֶר לָהּ הֻגֵּד הֻגַּד לִי כֹּל אֲשֶׁר־עָשִׂית אֶת־חֲמוֹתֵךְ אַחֲרֵי מוֹת אִישֵׁךְ וַתַּעַזְבִי אָבִיךְ וְאִמֵּךְ וְאֶרֶץ מוֹלַדְתֵּךְ וַתֵּלְכִי אֶל־עַם אֲשֶׁר לֹא־יָדַעַתְּ תְּמוֹל שִׁלְשׁוֹם:

Boaz answered and said to her, "It has been fully related to me all that you have done for your mother-in-law after the death of your husband, and how you left your father and your mother and the land of your birth and went to a people that you did not know yesterday or the day before."

Boaz replied that, in view of what he had heard about her from many sources, his kindness was a small part of his obligation.

The double verb הֻגֵּד הֻגַּד, "it has been fully related," imparts that he had heard two things. First, she had dealt kindly with her mother-in-law, and as Naomi's relation he was obligated to requite the kindness. Second, she had left the security of family and the luxury of the royal palace to come to a strange land. Since she had never before seen the land or its people, that could not possibly have been what attracted her away from her native country. Obviously, then, her conversion was sincerely motivated by love of God.

The iterated הֻגֵּד הֻגַּד further indicates that he had heard of her good

Ruth 2

qualities in two areas: her kindness to Naomi at home, and her wisdom, modesty, and industriousness in the fields.

Now the term ויען can mean "raised his voice" as well as "answered"; that is, Boaz praised her loudly for all to hear. "You are not a stranger," he declared. "Your good qualities, particularly your kindness, make you one of us."

Boaz singled out the quality of kindness, for that is the essence of all good qualities. Our sages teach: A bride whose eyes are beautiful needs no further inspection. That is, a person who has עין טובה, "a benevolent eye," needs no further inspection to establish the excellence of his character.

Targum Yonathan explains the double הֻגֵּד הֻגַּד as follows: "It has been told to me by the sages that only male Moabites are prohibited from marrying Jews, and it has been told to me prophetically that kings and prophets will descend from you in the merit of your kindness to your mother-in-law."

Moabite women in general, and she in particular, were permitted to marry Jews because the reason given by the Torah for the prohibition does not apply to them. The Moabites had failed to welcome the Israelites with bread and water, but it is not incumbent upon women to come out in greeting. Accordingly, they are excluded from the prohibition.

Indeed, by treating her mother-in-law kindly and even supporting her, Ruth did the opposite of what her ungenerous forefathers had done.

Only three days prior to Ruth's arrival, this question had been put to the sages, and they had just replied: "We have a tradition from Sinai: a Moabite, not a Moabitess." Therefore Boaz emphasized that she had not been in the land of Israel "yesterday or the day before." Had she come a day sooner, she would not have been accepted for marriage into the Jewish nation, since the halacha had only now been clarified.

2:12

יְשַׁלֵּם יְהֹוָה פָּעֳלֵךְ וּתְהִי מַשְׂכֻּרְתֵּךְ שְׁלֵמָה מֵעִם יְהֹוָה אֱלֹהֵי יִשְׂרָאֵל אֲשֶׁר־בָּאת לַחֲסוֹת תַּחַת־כְּנָפָיו:

"The Lord repay your deed, and be your reward complete from the Lord, God of Israel, beneath Whose wings you have come to shelter."

"Do not imagine that your reward ends with my kindness to you," said Boaz. "To requite your wonderful deeds is beyond human ability.

Your reward will come from God Who has great goodness hidden away for the righteous."

Since she was a woman alone in a strange land, Boaz blessed her according to her needs: with wealth and marriage.

The Targum translates: "May God repay you in this world for your good deeds, and may your reward be complete in the hereafter for coming to convert."

An act of kindness is like a loan made to God, as it is written, "He who is merciful to the poor lends to the Lord" (Proverbs 19:17). Thus, for her kindness to Naomi, God would "repay your deed."

In addition, her soul would shelter beneath the wings of God. Our sages observe that those who do acts of kindness take refuge not under the wings of the supernal *Hayyoth* that draw the Heavenly Chariot (Ezekiel 1), nor of the Cherubs, nor of the Seraphs, but under the wings of the Creator Himself.

"How precious is Your kindness, O God," exclaimed King David; "and the sons of man shelter in the shadow of Your wings" (Psalms 36:8). Human kindness is a pale imitation and reflection of divine kindness, and if in return for the kindness that a man does he merits to gain shelter beneath God's wings, how precious must God's own kindness be!

Moreover, since kindness yields dividends for the benefactor in this world even as the principal remains intact for him in the World to Come (Talmud), Boaz assured Ruth that she would enjoy the dividends of her kindness to Naomi in this world. Her children would become leaders of Israel and she herself would wear the royal crown. Although she was a pauper at the moment, her descendant would dedicate a hundred talents of gold to the Temple (Ezra 8:26). Her reward would be שְׁלֵמָה, "complete," which also spells שְׁלֹמֹה, Solomon, whom she would live to see, as it is written: "[Solomon] caused a throne to be set for the mother of the king" (1 Kings 2:19), that is, for the mother of royalty—Ruth.

These would be the dividends. The principal reward to come from the Lord, God of Israel, was reserved for her soul in the World to Come, where it would shelter under God's wings, "revel in the pleasantness of the Lord, and visit in His palace" (Psalms 27:4).

Rabbi Chassa accented the special sense of "beneath Whose wings you have come to shelter." Ruth's reward would be great not because of her good qualities and her kindness to her mother-in-law, but because she converted.

Boaz mentioned two rewards—"The Lord repay your deed," and "be

Ruth 2

your reward complete." A proselyte is rewarded for his resolution to accept the *mitzvoth* as well as for his actual conversion. Furthermore, because she hastened to come instead of tarrying as other converts do, her reward would be complete in both worlds. She would not suffer in this world as other converts do.

For coming to shelter under His wings willingly and sincerely, with no ulterior motives, and without hope of ever marrying, God would give her a boundless reward in the World to Come, where "the righteous sit with crowns on their heads and enjoy the radiance of the *Shechinah*" (Talmud).

Since the souls of the righteous of Israel reside above the wings of the *Shechinah* and the souls of the converts below, Ruth had converted with the idea of sheltering "beneath [His] wings." Boaz assured her, however, that her reward would be "complete," that is, her soul would reside above His wings together with the righteous of Israel.

Abraham was the first convert, and his protective merit extends to all future converts. But Ruth had no need to rely on his merit, for her action surpassed his. She was שלמה—her own merit was complete and inexhaustible.

While Abraham had come to the Holy Land at God's command to "go forth from your land, and from your birthplace, and from your father's house" (Genesis 12:1), Ruth came on her own initiative and against Naomi's protests. Her reward would be complete as if "you [singular] have come" alone, without Naomi.

That she sought shelter with the God of Israel was also its own reward, for the reward of a *mitzvah*, the Talmud teaches, is the *mitzvah* itself.

2:13 וַתֹּאמֶר אֶמְצָא־חֵן בְּעֵינֶיךָ אֲדֹנִי כִּי נִחַמְתָּנִי וְכִי דִבַּרְתָּ עַל־לֵב שִׁפְחָתֶךָ וְאָנֹכִי לֹא אֶהְיֶה כְּאַחַת שִׁפְחֹתֶיךָ:

She said, "May I find favor in your eyes, my lord, because you have comforted me, and because you have spoken to the heart of your maidservant, though I am not even (alt: though I shall not be) like one of your maidservants."

"In gratitude for your comforting words and your kind welcome, and for the honor you accorded me by deigning to speak to me, I will devote my entire life to being nothing else but (לא אהיה אלא) your handmaiden."

Aware that the Torah says: "An Ammonite or a Moabite shall not enter the congregation of God" (Deuteronomy 23:4), Ruth thought that her status would not even equal that of a freed Canaanite maidservant: "I shall not be like one of your maidservants." And Boaz had comforted her by declaring it permissible for her to enter God's congregation.

Moreover, he had gladdened her heart by assuring her a share in the World to Come together with the righteous.

Or else, Ruth protested that she was not even as righteous as one of his maidservants. Although our sages assure even a maidservant in the land of Israel of a share in the World to Come, Ruth thought herself unworthy of it, let alone meritorious of a portion with the righteous.

Then she added: "Before you spoke to me so kindly I would not have dared ask you for anything. Now that you have been kind to me and comforted me, I ask to find favor in your eyes in the future as a member of your household, although I am not worthy of being even of your maidservants."

Just as Abigail was to say, "May you remember your maidservant" (1 Samuel 25:31) to hint that David wed her, possibly too Ruth said, "May I find favor in your eyes" to hint that Boaz should wed her. For "a woman's favor," our sages declare, "is upon her husband"; it is measured by the man's willingness to marry her.

Conversely, the scripture says, "if it comes to pass that she does not find favor in his eyes ... he shall send her forth out of his house" (Deuteronomy 24:1).

Ruth hoped he would wed her because she found "favor in your eyes" even if she was unworthy. Indeed, from his comforting words it appeared that she would "not be like one of your maidservants," but his wife and the mainstay of his home.

2:14 וַיֹּאמֶר לָה בֹעַז לְעֵת הָאֹכֶל גֹּשִׁי הֲלֹם וְאָכַלְתְּ מִן־הַלֶּחֶם וְטָבַלְתְּ פִּתֵּךְ בַּחֹמֶץ וַתֵּשֶׁב מִצַּד הַקֹּצְרִים וַיִּצְבָּט־לָהּ קָלִי וַתֹּאכַל וַתִּשְׂבַּע וַתֹּתַר׃

And Boaz said to her at mealtime, "Approach hither, and eat of the bread and dip your morsel in the vinegar." So she sat at the side of the reapers. He handed her parched grain, and she ate, and was satisfied, and left over.

Ruth 2

How great is the power of gratitude! No sooner had she said, "May I find favor in the eyes of my lord" than he doubled his kindness and began to care for all her needs.

The word לָהּ, "to her," is curiously missing the usual *mapik* (dot) in the letter *heh* (ה). Our sages therefore render the word as לֹא, not. "No," said Boaz, "you are not of the maidservants, as you have said, but of the matriarchs who built the house of Israel."

Similarly, the *mapik* in the *heh* is missing in the verse, "He called it (לה) Novach in his name" (Numbers 32:42), for the name (Novach) did not last. And here (v. 14), the missing *mapik* hints likewise that Boaz's marriage to Ruth would not endure. The night he wed her, he died.

It also conveys that he did not speak directly "to her," but to all the women gleaning in the field, to keep above suspicion. For the same reason, he spoke to her "at mealtime," when courtesy demanded that he invite her to join the others in the reapers' repast; and he gave her only a little. Furthermore, he did not ask her to come "here" (הֲנָה), close to the men, but simply to partake of the meal, hence the unusual term הֲלֹם, "hither."

According to a different interpretation, "at mealtime" is part of Boaz's statement. "Each day at mealtime," he said, "come here to eat; you need not wait to be invited."

In the manner of the good host, Boaz urged her to partake, adding that her joining the meal would cause no trouble or expense. Enough bread had already been prepared, and vinegar was inexpensive and abundant. Let her then consider the bread as her own ("your morsel").

Seeing her hesitate, he added, "If you prefer not to eat of the reapers' meal, eat your own bread and dip it in our vinegar."

The sages remark upon the fact that usually guests are not invited to partake of vinegar. However, Boaz feared that Ruth, a king's daughter, was unaccustomed to the strong sun and might suffer sunstroke. So he advised her to dip her bread in vinegar, which protects against the heat.

Targum Yonathan translates: "You shall dip your bread in food which has been cooked with vinegar."

In deference to Boaz's wishes, Ruth sat "at the side of the reapers." She did not come near them, or partake of the food, so he graciously handed her some "parched grain" (קָלִי) of his own meal.

Our sages explain קָלִי not as a kind of food but as referring to the quantity. Since he had said, "dip your morsel in vinegar," yet the verse does not mention that he gave her bread, they render קָלִי as a "pinch," cognate of קְלִיל, a little. He handed her a bit of food.

Rabbi Yitzchak said: Either the fingers of that righteous man or the stomach of that righteous woman were blessed, for he gave her only a pinch, but she "was satisfied, and left over."

The Talmud says: If a person performs a *mitzvah*, he should perform it wholeheartedly. Had Boaz known that God would write of him, "He offered her a pinch," he would have served her fatted calves.

The simple meaning of this statement is that a good cause deserves maximum effort; one should not give sparingly, as Boaz did.

On the other hand, the scripture testifies that he gave generously enough so that she "ate, and was satisfied, and left over." And the only reason Boaz did not serve her fatted calves was to avoid suspicion. Had he known, however, that the scripture would place him above suspicion by recording his deed, fatted calves he would indeed have served her. As it was, he acted wholeheartedly, though imperfectly, and God who "seeks the heart" recorded the deed as if it were perfect.

This is a pattern which recurs in the Holy Scripture. Reuben influenced his brothers with words; Aaron was righteous in thought: he rejoiced in his heart; Boaz accented the deed. And in regard to all three God had to testify to their good intentions.

Reuben said, "Let us go and throw him into the pit" (Genesis 37:22) that swarmed with snakes and scorpions, although his intention was to save Joseph from his brothers' hands. For he was afraid that if he asked for more, they would kill him as well. Reuben's deed was flawed, for without a miracle to save him, Joseph would have perished in the pit. But his intention was to save him, and he did not carry him on his shoulders only because he was afraid that he would not succeed. Had he known what the scripture would record, he would have tried to return him to his father in the knowledge that he would succeed. Although the deed was not perfect, being limited to words, the scripture writes, "He saved him from their hands" (Genesis 37:21).

Similarly, Aaron kissed Moses (Exodus 4:27), yet God had to testify to his generous feelings. Aaron did not come out to greet Moses with music and dance because he feared that people would say that it was meant to cover up the jealousy in his heart. Had he known that the scripture would testify to his joy at his brother's good fortune, he would have done so. Although the deed was flawed, being confined to his thought, the scripture writes of it as if it were perfect. This indicates that purity of motive is most important.

The righteous promise little but do much. Abraham said to the angels who visited him, "Let me take a loaf of bread" (Genesis 18:5), but brought them cream and milk, followed by meat (Talmud). Similarly, Boaz told Ruth to "eat of the bread," but then "handed her parched grain," which "she ate," followed by an array of delicacies, from which she "was satisfied." Moreover, he served her more than she could eat, so that she "left over."

According to the Midrash, he said, ["Approach to the royalty." Thus the term הֲלֹם was later used to refer to kingship: "Who am I . . . that you have brought me הֲלֹם, hither" (2 Samuel 7:18).] "You shall eat of the bread of royalty, dipped in the vinegar of suffering that inevitably accompanies it."

Thus one of the kings to descend from her would be like harsh vinegar, although the son of wine—Manasseh, the wicked son of the righteous King Chizkiyah.

The unusual word ויצבט, "he handed her," is seen as being composed of two words, ויצב ט, "nine stood," alluding to the nine kings that would descend from her: David, Solomon, Asa, Yehoshafat, Uziah, Yotam, Chizkiyah, Yosiah, and Amatziah (or else the Messiah).

2:15 וַתָּקָם לְלַקֵּט וַיְצַו בֹּעַז אֶת־נְעָרָיו לֵאמֹר גַּם בֵּין הָעֳמָרִים תְּלַקֵּט וְלֹא תַכְלִימוּהָ:

Then she rose to glean. And Boaz instructed his men, saying, "Let her glean even among the sheaves; and do not embarrass (alt: prevent) her."

Although Boaz had spoken kindly to her and served her from his table, she did not rely on his support. Having finished eating, she immediately "rose to glean," without stopping to rest after the meal and without waiting for the reapers to return to work.

In doing so, she also avoided attracting attention to herself from any of the workers.

The gladdening words she had heard from Boaz raised her spirits. She rose just as Jacob had "picked up his legs" (Genesis 29:1) after having heard good news.

When she was out of earshot, Boaz instructed his men to be kind and let her glean among the sheaves. By not doing so in her presence, he impressed upon them the sincerity of his words.

Paupers were generally not permitted to pick among the sheaves, lest they take stalks out of the sheaves themselves. When therefore the overseer had implied that Ruth was picking from among the sheaves (v. 7), Boaz instructed his workers that if she picked from among the heaps, and even took from the bound sheaves, to which she was not entitled, they should not stop her.

He ensured that plenty of grain would be available for her to pick, but emphasized "let her glean." He would not give it to her, lest it be misconstrued as the gift that effects a marriage bond.

Another interpretation is that Boaz instructed his workers לֵאמֹר, that is, to say to her that she should pick among the sheaves. She would then not be embarrassed to do so.

2:16 וְגַם שֹׁל־תָּשֹׁלּוּ לָהּ מִן־הַצְּבָתִים וַעֲזַבְתֶּם וְלִקְּטָה וְלֹא תִגְעֲרוּ־בָהּ:

"Also pull out [stalks] for her from the heaps; then leave and let her pick. And do not rebuke her."

To ensure Ruth an abundant supply of barley without compromising her pride, Boaz instructed his men to create "leket" and "shikechah" for her to pick—"leket" by pulling ears out of the sheaves and scattering them about, and "shikechah" by pretending to forget sheaves. He emphasized that this was to be done "for her," that is, in a way that she would be sure to acquire the grain. When they saw her coming they were quickly to prepare some "leket" and "shikechah," and then "leave and let her pick."

The verb שֹׁל may be translated as forget, cast down, or drop off—as in שַׁל נְעָלֶיךָ, "cast off your shoes" (Exodus 3:5), or כִּי יִשַּׁל זֵיתֶךָ, "your olives will drop off" (Deuteronomy 28:40), or to give booty (שלל). The term צְבָתִים may mean small sheaves, which can easily be used for this subterfuge, or large sheaves, which do not come under the ruling of *shikechah*.

The double verb שׁל תשלו indicates that the action was to be repeated many times.

In resorting to these ruses to support her without her knowledge, Boaz was fulfilling the commandment of charity *par excellence*. By giving secretly to spare the poor embarrassment, he emulated God Who sustains the world בחן בחסד וברחמים, with pleasantness as well as kindness and mercy (from Grace after Meals).

The Mishnah teaches that a landowner who allows one pauper to pick but not another, or who helps only one of them, is robbing the poor. The reason is that other paupers might stay away when they see that he favors that one. Boaz therefore contrived to benefit Ruth in an area beyond the legal rights of the poor: among the sheaves and with *shikechah* that was deliberately "forgotten."

It was also because of Ruth's incredible beauty that Boaz instructed his men not to help her pick, but to "leave and let her pick," lest they come to sinful thoughts.

Although Boaz had already admonished his workers to "let her pick" among the sheaves (v. 15), he now repeated the admonition to be sure they complied. According to a different interpretation, previously he had spoken of עמרים, bundles of stalks as yet untied; now he referred to צבתים, bound sheaves, or else grain ready for beating, as in ויצבט לה קלי (v. 14).

Should Ruth, after the special arrangements he had made for her, take even more, or pick together with the other paupers, the workers were not to stop her.

He further admonished them to speak to her gently, as befits a princess. And thus he upheld the teaching of our sages that the Torah prohibition against afflicting another (Leviticus 25:17) refers to verbal abuse.

Boaz earned the kingship of the house of David by speaking gently to Ruth. And in him there came true, "The Lord your God will bless you," which the Torah accords to those who fulfill the commandments of *leket*, *shikechah*, and *peah* "for the stranger, the fatherless, and the widow" (Deuteronomy 24:19).

2:17 וַתְּלַקֵּט בַּשָּׂדֶה עַד־הָעָרֶב וַתַּחְבֹּט אֵת אֲשֶׁר־לִקֵּטָה וַיְהִי כְּאֵיפָה שְׂעֹרִים:

She gleaned in the field until the evening. Then she beat out what she had gleaned, and it was about an *ephah* of barley.

In compliance with Boaz's instructions not to pick in other fields,

Ruth remained in "the field" of Boaz, picking the *leket*. She did not gather *shikechah*, for she perceived that the reapers were "forgetting" sheaves for her sake, and she would not accept charity from Boaz. Nevertheless, Boaz's reapers left her so much *leket* that she did not finish gathering it all until evening.

When at last she finished, she did not go home immediately to rest from her hard day's work, but first beat out her grain, both to spare Naomi the labor and to lighten the load she would have to carry in to the city.

The combined result of Boaz's generosity, Ruth's industriousness, and God's blessing was that in a single day she had gathered the remarkable quantity of an *ephah* of barley—a ten-day food supply. (An *ephah* is ten *omer* or three *seah*.)

2:18 וַתִּשָּׂא וַתָּבוֹא הָעִיר וַתֵּרֶא חֲמוֹתָהּ אֵת אֲשֶׁר־לִקֵּטָה וַתּוֹצֵא וַתִּתֶּן־לָהּ אֵת אֲשֶׁר־הוֹתִרָה מִשָּׂבְעָהּ:

She carried [it] and came to the city. Her mother-in-law saw what she had gleaned; and she took out and gave her what she had left over after eating her fill.

Having beaten out the grain, Ruth was able to carry the entire *ephah* into the city in a single trip with no assistance. Although her burden was heavy, happiness made her feet light, and she went directly home to avoid contact with undesirable elements.

Upon her arrival, Ruth did not show off her pickings. Naomi "saw" (ותרא) for herself, and was pleased (another meaning of ותרא) with the quality and quantity of "what she had gleaned" and with the fact that Ruth had already beaten it out.

Realizing that Naomi felt sorry about having nothing to serve her daughter-in-law when she came home hungry and tired from the field, Ruth immediately "took out ... what she had left over after eating her fill" and told Naomi that she had already eaten well in the field. Although she was tired from the long trek home, Ruth "gave her" the food to eat before eating herself.

Naomi was astonished at the quantity Ruth had picked, and her astonishment was compounded when Ruth gave her the leftovers of the meal in the field, for it showed that there, too, she had been blessed. A little food had been more than enough to satiate her.

2:19 וַתֹּאמֶר לָהּ חֲמוֹתָהּ אֵיפֹה לִקַּטְתְּ הַיּוֹם וְאָנָה עָשִׂית יְהִי מַכִּירֵךְ בָּרוּךְ וַתַּגֵּד לַחֲמוֹתָהּ אֵת אֲשֶׁר־עָשְׂתָה עִמּוֹ וַתֹּאמֶר שֵׁם הָאִישׁ אֲשֶׁר עָשִׂיתִי עִמּוֹ הַיּוֹם בֹּעַז:

Her mother-in-law said to her, "Where have you picked today and where have you wrought? May your benefactor be blessed."

She told her mother-in-law for whom she had wrought, and she said, "The name of the man for whom I wrought [by whom I worked] today is Boaz."

Astonished at the amount of clean grain Ruth had brought home, Naomi spoke quickly and excitedly, the thoughts tumbling out one after another.

"Where did you pick so much grain?" she asked. "What field owner gave you a free hand to pick, treated you with dignity, and even allowed you the rare privilege of beating out your grain in his field? Blessed be the one who welcomed you as if he were מַכִּירֵךְ, your friend or relative."

[Naomi's second question, ואנה עשית, is generally explained as referring to Ruth rather than to her benefactor.]

"How long (עד אנא)—as in עד אנה ינאצוני, 'how long will [this people] despise me?' (Numbers 14:11)—did it take you to pick all of this?" To which Ruth replied, "היום, all day."

"In one day it is impossible to gather so much grain through *peah*, *leket*, and *shikechah*. Did you perhaps work for wages?" And Ruth answered that she had worked for Boaz, who already had many workers and evidently hired her out of kindness.

"You have garnered much grain! You are truly a woman of valor who eats not the bread of idleness (Proverbs 31:27), and you will be a blessing to the man who will take notice of you and become your husband."

Ruth modestly objected, however, that the credit went not to her industriousness but to the extraordinary generosity of Boaz.

Recognizing God's blessing in the abundance of grain, Naomi wondered whether it had come on account of the righteous Ruth or the generosity of her benefactor. In case the blessing had come because of Ruth, she asked, "Where have you picked, so that I may pray that the benefactor be blessed as well?" And if it had been on account of the owner of the field, she asked "Where have you wrought?" Ruth modestly replied that it had come on account of Boaz, for "the generous of eye shall be blessed" (Proverbs 22:9).

Or else, realizing that Ruth could not have simply picked so much, Naomi concluded that she must have accepted the gift of מכירך, a relative, and Naomi blessed him for his generosity.

Ruth named the field owner, but tactfully pretended not to know he was a relative in order to play down the embarrassing fact that Naomi's kinsman had seen her daughter-in-law picking with the paupers.

Our sages note that instead of saying that Boaz had wrought for her, Ruth spoke of "the man for whom I wrought." They thus infer that "More than the householder does for the pauper, the pauper does for the householder." For in return for the charity he gives, the householder receives God's blessing.

Furthermore, from the verse, "Deal your bread to the hungry, and the cast-out poor bring to your home" (Isaiah 58:7), our sages conclude that if a householder is worthy, his charity goes to the hungry and saves lives; if not, it goes to the less poor. Since Naomi and Ruth had arrived in Bethlehem on the point of starvation, Ruth's benefactor had acquired the merit of saving a life, and was sure to be greatly blessed.

When therefore Ruth identified Boaz as her benefactor, Naomi exclaimed, "Thank God that he was the one so privileged!"

2:20 וַתֹּאמֶר נָעֳמִי לְכַלָּתָהּ בָּרוּךְ הוּא לַיהוָה אֲשֶׁר לֹא־עָזַב חַסְדּוֹ אֶת־הַחַיִּים וְאֶת־הַמֵּתִים וַתֹּאמֶר לָהּ נָעֳמִי קָרוֹב לָנוּ הָאִישׁ מִגֹּאֲלֵנוּ הוּא׃

Naomi said to her daughter-in-law, "Blessed is he of the Lord, who has not left off his kindness to the living and to the dead."

Naomi said to her, "The man is related to us; he is one of our redeemers."

"It is not within our power to repay him for all that he has done for us. May then God Who is ever kind to the living and the dead never cease to bless Boaz for his kindness."

She added, "There is a reason that Boaz showed you special kindness. He is our kin and redeemer, and has also dealt kindly with my deceased husband and sons."

According to a different interpretation, Naomi said: "I blessed your benefactor (v. 19) before I knew his identity. Boaz has no need of my blessing; he is already blessed of God for his constant practice of charity and kindness. His kindness to you today will continue," she added, "for not only is it his way to extend kindness and generosity to strangers, but the Torah has said that helping next-of-kin takes precedence."

Thus it is written, "If you lend money to *any* of My people, *even* to the poor with you . . ." (Exodus 22:24). And our sages elaborate: "The poor who are with you"—your own kin—come first.

"The obligation of redeemer," she concluded, "therefore rests upon him."

His kindness to the living is also a kindness to the dead, who are affected according to the fortune or misfortune of their living relatives. By supporting "the living" Naomi and Ruth, Boaz had spared "the dead" Elimelech and Machlon the shame of having their widows starve or pick in the fields of strangers. Nor was it demeaning for Ruth to pick in the field of Boaz, who was a relative and redeemer.

Ruth, however, failed to understand fully what Naomi meant by Boaz's kindness "to the dead," and Naomi explained that he was a "redeemer"; he would wed Ruth to perpetuate the name of her deceased husband.

This marriage would also redeem "the living" (plural). Naomi and Ruth will both fulfill their designated purpose—when Ruth bears Boaz a child and "there is born a son to Naomi" (v. 4:17). For this child would be the forebear of Israel's redeemer.

Said Rabbi Shmuel ben Nachmani: "Boaz was the leading sage of the generation and the woman made of him a relative." That is, at first the families of Elimelech and of Naomi had been greater than the family of Boaz, and worthy of kingship; hence Boaz was called *their* relative, as Naomi said, "The man is related to us." The kinship was to his advantage. Now, however, they had sunk to such straits that they needed him to redeem them, and Naomi concluded, "He is one of our redeemers."

2:21

וַתֹּאמֶר רוּת הַמּוֹאֲבִיָּה גַּם כִּי־אָמַר אֵלַי עִם־הַנְּעָרִים אֲשֶׁר־לִי תִּדְבָּקִין עַד אִם־כִּלּוּ אֵת כָּל־הַקָּצִיר אֲשֶׁר־לִי:

Ruth the Moabite said, "He even said to me, 'Stay close to my young men until they have finished the harvest.'"

At first Ruth had refrained from telling Naomi of Boaz's invitation to stay in the field, lest Naomi suspect him of dishonorable intentions. But now that Naomi told her he was a relative, Ruth revealed that he had given her permission to pick in his field for the entire harvest season. She used the unusual phrase עד אם כלו, literally, "Until *if* they have finished," to express uncertainty, since one never knows what the future will bring.

Coming from a stingy people, "the Moabite" marveled at the generosity of Boaz, and when Naomi blessed him for his kindness, Ruth enthusiastically added, "That is not all—he even assured my safety in his field, where all the workers are righteous."

According to the view that he had appointed her overseer, this was in keeping with Torah law, since the prohibition of *yichud* (seclusion of men and women) does not apply to two righteous men in the company of a woman. "Stay close to my young men..." was thus Ruth's paraphrasing of Boaz's statement: "Keep your eyes on the field that they will harvest, and walk after them. Have I not ordered them not to touch you" (v. 9).

Most commentators note that Boaz had specifically stressed "Stay here close to my girls" (v. 8), whereas Ruth reported him as saying, "Stay close to my young men." Rabbi Chanan bar Levi said: She is certainly a Moabite, for he said, "Stay close to my girls," but she said, "to my young men."

That is, since the prohibition of *yichud* was new to Ruth, coming as she had from the licentious Moabites, she did not think of emphasizing that the workers with whom she was to stay were female.

Or else it was simply a grammatical error by a Moabite for whom Hebrew was a new language [saying נערים instead of נערות].

A different interpretation is that she deliberately changed his words to avoid giving Naomi the impression that Boaz had told her to stay with the women because she had behaved improperly.

The Targum resolves the difficulty by translating נערים as children reared in the Torah way of life to keep the *mitzvoth*. Ruth was to stay with them when not actually picking grain.

2:22 וַתֹּאמֶר נָעֳמִי אֶל־רוּת כַּלָּתָהּ טוֹב בִּתִּי כִּי תֵצְאִי עִם־נַעֲרוֹתָיו וְלֹא יִפְגְּעוּ־בָךְ בְּשָׂדֶה אַחֵר:

Naomi said to her daughter-in-law Ruth, "It is good, my daughter, that you go out with his young women, and that you be not molested in another field."

When Ruth told her of Boaz's invitation to stay with his men, Naomi gently corrected her by saying, "It is good ... that you go out with his young women."

Although his men were righteous, and there is no prohibition of *yichud* with several righteous men, whom Boaz had moreover specifically instructed not to touch her, nevertheless it was better for her to remain with his girls. Indeed, had not Boaz himself told her to remain with his men "until they have finished the harvest" (v. 2:21), because after that he could no longer guarantee her safety!

In particular, Ruth was to "go out" of the field in the girls' company to avoid gossip. Not everyone would recognize the men as being Boaz's righteous workers.

Naomi, however, agreed that Ruth should stay in Boaz's field until the end of the harvest season rather than go to "another field," where less righteous men might molest her. Nor would they receive her as graciously as did Boaz, who had entreated her to remain in his field.

In this regard, the term יפגעו, literally "encounter," also means to entreat, as in אל תפגעי בי לעזבך, "Entreat me not to leave you" (v. 1:16).

"Even if you are entreated to go elsewhere, do not listen. Stay in the field of Boaz, where women are also present."

2:23 וַתִּדְבַּק בְּנַעֲרוֹת בֹּעַז לְלַקֵּט עַד־כְּלוֹת קְצִיר־הַשְּׂעֹרִים וּקְצִיר הַחִטִּים וַתֵּשֶׁב אֶת־חֲמוֹתָהּ:

So she cleaved to Boaz's young women to glean until the end of the barley harvest and the wheat harvest. Then she dwelt with her mother-in-law.

Throughout the three-month harvest season, Ruth picked all day and slept by night in the field with Boaz's young women. She probably acquired many new young friends, but her thoughts cleaved to her mother-in-law as if she dwelt together with her.

According to a different interpretation, Ruth "cleaved to Boaz's young women" only "to glean." Every evening she trudged back to the city so that Naomi would not be alone, and she did not abandon her bitter old mother-in-law for the company of happy young friends.

Naomi, seeing Ruth's steadfast devotion, decided to arrange a match for her with Boaz. But first the mandatory three-month waiting period before a convert may marry would have to elapse.

The harvest season drew to a close, and with it the convert's waiting period, but Ruth "dwelt with her mother-in-law," and made no effort to seek a husband.

RUTH 3

3:1 וַתֹּאמֶר לָהּ נָעֳמִי חֲמוֹתָהּ בִּתִּי הֲלֹא אֲבַקֶּשׁ־לָךְ מָנוֹחַ אֲשֶׁר יִיטַב־לָךְ:

Naomi, her mother-in-law, said to her, "My daughter, shall I not seek for you secure rest that it may be well with you?"

Both women had correctly surmised that Ruth found favor in the eyes of Boaz, who had recognized in her the woman from whom the line of David would come.

"A woman of valor who can find?" Solomon was to proclaim. "Her value is far beyond pearls" (Proverbs 31:10). But Boaz did not pursue his find. Three months had passed from the time of Ruth's conversion at the beginning of the harvest season, and still he made no move to seek her hand. It was as if after finding her, he lost her, and was resigned to the loss.

Naomi now took the initiative. A woman of valor herself, she "opened her mouth with wisdom" (Proverbs 31:26) and spoke to Ruth in a way that was beneficial and pleasant, as befit her name (*naomi*, the pleasant).

"Although Boaz has not broached the matter," she began, "I cannot rest until I see you secure in a marriage that will be good for you now and in years to come. Have I not advised you in the past to find rest, 'each in the house of her husband' (v. 1:9)? For a man has no peace without a wife, nor a woman without a husband."

For "marriage" Naomi used the term *manoach* (מָנוֹחַ), rest or security, which is also cognate with *nachat ruach*, spiritual satisfaction.

After death dissolved the family ties between Ruth and Naomi, and they remained destitute, purity of character bound them together. Ruth continued to treat Naomi as "her mother-in-law," and Naomi now set aside her bitterness over her own suffering to seek happiness—and a marriage partner—for Ruth. She was determined to find Ruth a "secure rest that it may be well with you," in contrast with her ill-fated marriage to Machlon.

"Although I am your mother-in-law," she said, "I seek your welfare as if you were my daughter. I advise you to marry an old man not because he is wealthy, but because he is a great *tzaddik* and the union will be good for you. As for me, although I will remain alone, I will rejoice in your happiness."

To underscore her words, Naomi swore to Ruth that she genuinely wished her to remarry. According to Targum Yonathan, the term הֲלוֹא, "shall I not," connotes an oath.

Naomi spoke of a rest that "may be" good for her—i.e., only in the future, seemingly—because the marriage would last but a few hours before Boaz died. The satisfaction that Ruth derived from the marriage came much later, when she saw her descendant King Solomon judging Israel, as it is written, "And [Solomon] had a chair set for the king's mother" (1 Kings 2:19). That was Ruth—the mother of royalty (Talmud).

The term *manoach*, security or rest, alludes to Solomon, who found rest from his enemies and who built the *Beth HaMikdash*, the earthly resting place of the Divine Presence (*Shechinah*). Thus he was to declare, "Now the Lord, my God, has given me rest on every side; there is neither adversary nor evil occurrence. And behold, I propose to build a house for the name of the Lord, my God" (1 Kings 5:18,19).

The word *manoach* further hints that the fruit of the marriage would be Menachem (the comforter)—the Messiah.

To allay Ruth's fear that none would deign to marry a mere convert like herself, Naomi reminded her of the teaching of our sages that a man can find happiness in marriage if he marries a woman of lower station. The right man would thus choose her.

3:2 וְעַתָּה הֲלֹא בֹעַז מֹדַעְתָּנוּ אֲשֶׁר הָיִית אֶת־נַעֲרוֹתָיו הִנֵּה־הוּא זֹרֶה אֶת־גֹּרֶן הַשְּׂעֹרִים הַלָּיְלָה׃

"And now is there not our kinsman Boaz, with whose young women you have been? Behold, he is winnowing barley on the threshing floor tonight."

"The best husband for you," continued Naomi, "is Boaz. He is a man of personal distinction, renowned throughout the land for his righteousness; and he is our relative, of the same aristocratic family as your late husband. Moreover, unlike those men of wealth who pretend not to know their poor kinfolk, he has continued to conduct himself as our kinsman. This you know from your own experience, having been with his young women. And you may have also come to know his nobility of character."

At the same time, Naomi was certain that Boaz would agree to wed Ruth. Not only was he a relative, but he had come to know her virtues by observing her in the field, and had already begun to show her kindness.

"Tonight," said Naomi, "is the time to act on my plan. He will be alone on the threshing floor, and full of joy after measuring the first bounteous crop after years of famine. Do not fear to approach him, for he is our kinsman and he knows you well from the field."

Naomi knew that Boaz would be sleeping on the threshing floor this night, because winnowing was done late in the day to avoid the sun's scorching rays, and was customarily followed by measuring the clean grain. In the meantime night would fall, and since, as the Talmud says, it is unseemly for a scholar to go out alone at night, Boaz would sleep on the threshing floor. Thereby he would also guard his grain from the thieves. He did not rely on his field hands to do this, for in those times harlots were paid from the threshing floor, which he wanted to avoid.

According to the Midrash, Boaz was then cutting the *omer*, an offering of barley that was cut at night and then winnowed.

Many generations earlier, when Rebekah had instructed Jacob to obtain from his father the blessing that Isaac had meant for Esau, Jacob had been reluctant to go, fearing that he would incur his father's curse instead. But Rebekah had insisted: "Tonight the treasures of dew are open, and the angels are singing God's praise. This is the night that your descendants will be redeemed from slavery, and this night they will sing the Song of Moses. Go then and prepare delicacies for your father so that he will bless you."

Similarly, when Naomi instructed Ruth to go to Boaz, Ruth was reluctant, and feared that she would incur his curse. But Naomi assured her that "now" was the time to act. For "tonight" he would be glad in spirit, and divine inspiration would rest upon him.

3:3 וְרָחַצְתְּ וָסַכְתְּ וְשַׂמְתְּ שמלתך (שִׂמְלֹתַיִךְ קרי) עָלַיִךְ וירדתי (וְיָרַדְתְּ קרי) הַגֹּרֶן אַל־תִּוָּדְעִי לָאִישׁ עַד כַּלֹּתוֹ לֶאֱכֹל וְלִשְׁתּוֹת:

"Therefore bathe, and anoint yourself, and put your raiment upon you, and go down to the threshing floor. Do not make yourself known to the man until he has finished eating and drinking."

Naomi asked Ruth to prepare for her mission as one prepares for the Sabbath: by bathing, anointing herself, and donning her Sabbath attire.

According to another interpretation, Ruth possessed only one shabby garment, which Naomi told her to arrange neatly, perhaps to roll it down as the halacha advises those who have no Sabbath garments. "If you arrange your garment neatly," Naomi assured her, "your appearance will be finer than if you were wearing costly robes, which in any case would be out of place on the threshing floor."

Our sages elaborate that Naomi's instructions relate to spiritual matters:

ורחצת—"Cleanse yourself of idolatry." Although Ruth had long since abandoned idolatry, she had not yet undergone the required ritual immersion before a conversion court of three judges. For upon arriving in Bethlehem she had immediately gone to pick in the field and worked straight through the harvest season. Or else, she had already immersed, and Naomi now simply warned her to shun pagan customs and superstitions. Thus our sages also explain ורחצת as "purify your soul," a step that follows conversion.

וסכת—"Annoint yourself with *mitzvoth* and charity." "Meticulously fulfill in detail every precept," Naomi admonished. "Even after you rise in social standing through your marriage to Boaz, do not become haughty, but continue your careful observance."

In this regard her "donning Sabbath attire" alludes to spiritual matters, since our sages characterize the Sabbath as "an aspect of the World to Come."

The word ושמת, meaning "put," is spelled ושמתי, "I will put," to convey Naomi's assurance that she herself would do the same. Similarly, וירדת, "go down," is spelled וירדתי, "I will go down." That is, Naomi's merit would accompany Ruth on her mission.

Naomi assured Ruth that no one would see her going, for the threshing sites were located in the lowest part of the city, which is most sheltered from the wind, so that the grain would not be blown away along with the chaff.

"Tonight Boaz will eat at length," said Naomi. "Do not risk irritating him by disturbing his meal, but wait patiently in your hiding place until he has finished. Then emerge stealthily and note where he lies down to sleep."

3:4 וִיהִ֣י בְשָׁכְב֗וֹ וְיָדַ֙עַתְּ֙ אֶת־הַמָּקוֹם֙ אֲשֶׁ֣ר יִשְׁכַּב־שָׁ֔ם וּבָ֛את וְגִלִּ֥ית מַרְגְּלֹתָ֖יו וְשָׁכָ֑בְתְּ וְה֣וּא יַגִּ֣יד לָ֔ךְ אֵ֖ת אֲשֶׁ֥ר תַּעֲשִֽׂין׃

"And it shall be when he lies down, that you will know the place where he lies. Then come and uncover his feet and lie down, and he will tell you what you are to do."

"Having already noted where he sleeps," continued Naomi, "you will be able to find him later [in the dark]. When he awakens, ask his advice, and he, in his wisdom, will tell you what to do."

If Naomi wished to arrange a match between Boaz and Ruth, the conventional approach would have been for her to speak to Boaz and suggest that as a relative and redeemer he wed Ruth, whom he personally knew to be a woman of valor. If the match was truly from God, the matter would have been successfully completed with minimal effort. Why did Naomi choose instead to expose Boaz to temptation? Why did she send Ruth down to the threshing floor to lie at the feet of Boaz, judge of Israel and head of the Sanhedrin, and ask him to marry her?

One answer is that had Naomi approached Boaz directly, he would have replied that Ruth would be happier as the wife of Plony Almony, a closer relative. But Naomi wanted the seed of Boaz to come through Ruth. She instructed Ruth to lie quietly at the feet of Boaz as a demonstration that her purpose was solely for the sake of heaven, and could be accomplished only through this aged sage and *tzaddik*.

Another answer is that Naomi was certain that Ruth was to be the mother of royalty, but did not know whether the father would be Boaz or another redeemer, perhaps even a member of a different Judean family. Therefore she avoided a direct approach, preferring to arrange matters so that the outcome would be entirely in the hand of God. For as our sages teach, God has been engaged in creating the light of the Messiah since the beginning of the world.

An early instance of God "creating the light of the Messiah" was when He sent an angel to rescue Lot and his two daughters from the destruction of Sodom. In the cave where they took refuge, the daughters plied Lot with wine that Providence provided, and consorted with him "so that we may give life to offspring through our father" (Genesis 19:32). The result—the nations of Moab and Ammon, who bore within them Messianic sparks waiting to enter Israel through two "pearls" of these nations.

Naomi's plan was to hint of the deed of Lot's daughters and bring

Boaz to the recognition that Ruth was the long-awaited "pearl of Moab."

Again, God was engaged in creating the light of the Messiah when Tamar, dressed as a harlot, lured Judah off the path and bore him Peretz, another link in the chain leading to David and the Messiah. Naomi chose to follow in her footsteps—as hinted at by the end letters of א׳ת המקום, אש׳ר, "the place where," which spell תמר, Tamar—for she was certain that through Ruth God would complete what Tamar had begun.

Esoterically, Naomi's actions were also a means to foil Satan, so to speak, similar to Israel "appeasing" Satan on Yom Kippur by sending the Seir Azazel to its destruction (Leviticus 16). Thus Jacob produced the twelve tribes by marrying two sisters, which Torah law forbids, Judah begot Peretz through an unconventional tryst with Tamar, and Ruth went to Boaz on the threshing floor, to appease Satan and foil his mission of preventing God's light from being brought into the world.

3:5 וַתֹּאמֶר אֵלֶיהָ כֹּל אֲשֶׁר־תֹּאמְרִי אֵלַי (קרי ולא כתיב) אֶעֱשֶׂה:

And she said to her, "All that you say [to me] I will do."

Although Ruth did not understand the reason for the strange plan, which ran counter to her sense of modesty and dignity, she agreed to do whatever Naomi said, certain that Naomi's instructions were אֵלַי, "to me," that is, for her benefit.

But אֵלַי, though pronounced, is not written in the text, to convey that even if Naomi's instructions had not been for her benefit and addressed directly to her, Ruth would have carried them out nevertheless—simply because Naomi had spoken.

Also conveyed by the missing אֵלַי, is that Ruth went on her mission only to fulfill Naomi's wish, not to gain anything for herself. It was as if Ruth had no personal stake in the outcome.

3:6 וַתֵּרֶד הַגֹּרֶן וַתַּעַשׂ כְּכֹל אֲשֶׁר־צִוַּתָּה חֲמוֹתָהּ:

So she went down to the threshing floor, and she did according to all that her mother-in-law had commanded her.

Ruth changed only one detail of her mother-in-law's instructions. Out of modesty, she postponed anointing herself and dressing up until after her arrival at the threshing floor [in order not to attract attention on the way there].

Otherwise, Ruth did everything that Naomi said or even hinted, including to purify herself of idolatry. Thus she did not simply do כל, all, but כְּכֹל, "according to all" that her mother-in-law bade her. This also conveys that with every action Ruth said to herself, "I am doing this to fulfill my mother-in-law's command."

The extra letter כ (in ככל), resembling a semicircle also hints that she went with the pure intention of begetting judges of the Sanhedrin, who would sit facing one another in a semicircle, reminiscent of half a threshing floor.

Moreover, Solomon would build the *Beth HaMikdash* on the threshing floor of Aravna, which David purchased and consecrated as a place of worship (2 Samuel 24).

3:7 וַיֹּאכַל בֹּעַז וַיֵּשְׁתְּ וַיִּיטַב לִבּוֹ וַיָּבֹא לִשְׁכַּב בִּקְצֵה הָעֲרֵמָה וַתָּבֹא בַלָּט וַתְּגַל מַרְגְּלֹתָיו וַתִּשְׁכָּב׃

Boaz ate and drank, and his heart was glad. He came to lie down at the end of the stack [of grain]. Then she came softly, uncovered his feet and lay down.

During the famine, even those fortunate enough to eat well never felt satisfied, and the wealthy Boaz had deliberately restricted his own eating in order to share in the communal suffering. But now, having winnowed his grain and beheld its abundance, "Boaz ate" his fill for the first time in years.

Then, in fulfillment of the Torah command: "You shall eat, and be satisfied, and bless the Lord, your God, for the good land that He has given you" (Deuteronomy 8:10), Boaz joyously thanked God for providing food, and his heart was gladdened by reciting the Grace after Meals and studying Torah.

Obviously it was not eating that gladdened his heart, for "a righteous man eats [only] to satisfy his soul" (Proverbs 13:25) [not to revel in feasts]. Nor would his heart have been merry with wine, for the pious

Ruth 3

take care to remain sober for reciting the Grace after Meals. Moreover, the scripture does not say that "his heart was glad with wine" as it does of Ahasuerus (Esther 1:10).

According to the Targum, Boaz thanked God for accepting his prayers and ending the famine. Indeed, וייטב לבו may allude to the blessing הטוב והמטיב, "Who is good and does good," which one pronounces when a boon is granted.

Then, so that Ruth would not be kept waiting, God arranged for Boaz to go to sleep immediately.

Out of modesty, he went off alone to "the end of the stack," far from his servants. There, the wealthy aristocrat lay humbly down on the floor. Thus his modesty and humility made possible the implementation of Naomi's plan, and Ruth came to him without being noticed.

After Boaz lay down, Ruth came בלט, softly, quietly, perhaps with [her face] wrapped, like Elijah who "wrapped his face in his mantle" (וַיָּלֶט פָּנָיו בְּאַדַּרְתּוֹ) (1 Kings 19:13).

The scripture also uses בָּלָט (1 Samuel 24:5) to describe David's remarkable entry into the cave after his enemy Saul, who was pursuing him. On that occasion David was able to cut a piece off Saul's mantle without being detected.

Ruth's entry into the threshing floor that Boaz was guarding against thieves was no less remarkable, particularly since he was not yet asleep but had only gone "to lie down." Yet she came undetected, as if invisible. In this vein, בלט is reminiscent of בלהטיהם, "with their sorcery" (Exodus 7:11).

According to a different interpretation, Boaz did not notice her approaching because, having drunk wine, he fell into a deep sleep. Thus he only became aware of her at midnight, as the next verse records.

3:8 וַיְהִי בַּחֲצִי הַלַּיְלָה וַיֶּחֱרַד הָאִישׁ וַיִּלָּפֵת וְהִנֵּה אִשָּׁה שֹׁכֶבֶת מַרְגְּלֹתָיו:

And it came to pass at midnight that the man was startled and turned about; and behold, a woman was lying at his feet.

Boaz slept deeply until midnight. Then, as the wine began to wear off, he tossed and turned (*vayilafet*, וילפת) in his sleep, or else stretched out, as in, "Samson clasped (וַיִּלְפֹּת, i.e., by stretching his arms and legs against) the two middle pillars" (Judges 16:23)—and was startled to encounter someone lying at his feet. He put out his hand and felt the head of a woman.

Boaz always rose at midnight for worship and Torah study, following a tradition of his fathers that was subsequently also handed down to his descendants. Thus David said, "At midnight I rise to thank You for Your statutes of righteousness" (Psalms 119:62).

But this particular midnight Boaz awoke to face a great test. He found himself overwhelmed by desire (וילפת can also mean "seized") which he did not know if he could master. The possibility of sinning so frightened him that his flesh turned soft as relish (לפת), and instinctively he held his head with his hands (וילפת) as one does when terror-stricken.

Another interpretation is that he tried to scream, but she held him tight (וילפת) until he regained his composure.

By focusing on the thought that at this very moment, at midnight, God enters the Garden of Eden with the righteous, he succeeded in overpowering his evil inclination. Thereby he joined the ranks of the righteous Joseph who refused the advances of his master's wife, and of Paltiel son of Layish, who placed a dagger between himself and Michal, daughter of Saul, who had previously been betrothed to David (1 Samuel 25:44).

The beginning of this verse marks the middle of the book of Ruth, symbolic of the fact that the epic events it records transpired in the middle of the night.

The expression "it came to pass at midnight" is found three times in the scripture. "It came to pass at midnight, that the Lord smote every first-born in Egypt" (Exodus 12:29); "And Samson arose at midnight, seized the doors of the gate of the city" (Judges 16:3); and "it came to pass at midnight that the man was startled and turned about." Common to all three instances is the onset of redemption or the gaining of freedom, for midnight is a time when prayers are answered. Moreover, all occurred on the night of Passover (Talmud).

Likewise the future redemption will occur on Passover בחצי הלילה, "at midnight," which has the same numerical value (=190) as קץ ("end"), the term designating the End of Days or Messianic era.

The term ויחרד, besides meaning "was startled," also alludes to a state of prophecy. Boaz had a vision of David smiting Israel's enemies, the Philistines and Amalekites, and he therefore asked her, "Who are you that from you will descend the redeemer of Israel?"

Ruth 3

Our sages elaborate: Behold, the purest of women was lying at his feet.

3:9 וַיֹּאמֶר מִי־אָתְּ וַתֹּאמֶר אָנֹכִי רוּת אֲמָתֶךָ וּפָרַשְׂתָּ כְנָפֶךָ עַל־אֲמָתְךָ כִּי גֹאֵל אָתָּה:

"Who are you?" he asked.

"I am Ruth, your handmaiden," she said. "Spread your wing (the corner of your cloak) over your handmaiden, for you are a redeemer."

After identifying herself as Ruth, she reminded Boaz of their conversation in the field. "I am not even like one of your maidservants" (v. 2:13) she had said, and he had corrected her: "You are not of the maidservants, but of the matriarchs." Then he had informed her that she was permitted to marry a Jew, and praised her for seeking refuge beneath God's wings.

"God's wings," she now said to him, "are the righteous, whose merit protects the world. Grant me therefore refuge beneath your wing."

At the time he had also said that her reward would be complete (שְׁלֵמָה), implying that from her would come Solomon (שְׁלֹמֹה). "Let your words now be fulfilled," she urged. "Your lineage, deeds, and renowned wisdom mark you as the father of Israel's redeemers. Delay not our marriage and the advent of Solomon."

Ruth had lain at his feet that night like a baby bird without a nest or a mother's wing to shelter it. As Naomi had hoped, this would arouse Boaz's compassion, providing an opportune moment to speak of her destiny. And now she asked him to "spread your wing" and shelter her in marriage.

This sheltering aspect of marriage is reflected in the custom of covering the bride (and in some places also the groom) with a prayer shawl (*talith*, טלית) as if by a nuptial canopy (*chupah*, חופה).

Another interpretation is that she asked him to wed her in the manner of the Israelite handmaiden—hence "over *your* handmaiden"; that is, with the spreading of a cloak. Thus the scripture says, "If she please not her master who had espoused her to himself, then shall he let her be redeemed; to sell her to a foreign people he shall have no power, seeing he had dealt deceitfully with her (*be-vigdo-va*, בְּבִגְדוֹ־בָהּ)" (Exodus

21:8). Upon this the Talmud elaborates: "Render it (בְּבִגְדוֹ) "with his garment," since he had spread his *talith* over her [in wedding her]."

According to our sages, he asked her, "What is your status? Are you single or married, permitted or forbidden?" Whereupon Ruth, fearing from his words that he could not master his inclination, said, "Let it be through *chupah* and *kiddushin* (proper marriage) and the seven blessings pronounced over the bride and groom, for my purpose is to restore the soul of Machlon to the world.

"My mother-in-law and I," she continued, "are forced to sell our inheritance, the field of my (late) husband Machlon, and it is incumbent upon you to buy it, as it is written: 'The redeemer who is related (next) to him shall come and redeem that which his brother had sold' (Leviticus 25:25). Acquire me, then, along with the field, so that the name Machlon will be remembered when I go to the field and people say, 'That is Machlon's wife.'"

She mentioned her mother-in-law because the law of redemption did not actually apply to Ruth herself, since she was a convert. Moreover, Torah law required him only to redeem the field (ibid.), not to marry the widow; hence the plea to acquire her along with the field.

Nonetheless, it was customary that if a man died without children, one of his relatives married the widow to produce offspring for the deceased. Thus the scripture says below: "The day you buy the field from the hand of Naomi, and from Ruth the Moabite, the wife of the deceased you have also bought" (v. 4:5).

Our sages remark upon the difference between the speech of the righteous and that of the wicked. In contrast to Potiphar's wife who brazenly demanded of Joseph to "lie with me" (Genesis 39:7), Ruth obliquely and modestly said, "Spread your wing over your handmaiden."

It may be surprising that Naomi advised her to say even this much, but she had good precedents. The matriarch Leah had gone out to greet her husband Jacob saying, "To me shall you come" (Genesis 30:16), and the scripture then records that "God harkened to Leah, and she conceived and bore Jacob a fifth son" (Genesis 30:17), thereby testifying to the purity of her intention to bear more tribes. Then again, Jacob had earlier said to Laban, "Give me my wife that I may come to her" (Genesis 29:21); and he said, our sages add, "When will I beget the twelve tribes?"

Similarly, Ruth asked Boaz to "Spread your wing over your handmaiden," a plea for the sake of heaven, to produce the kingdom of the house of David.

Boaz responded favorably, which raises the question why he, the leading sage of his generation, acted differently than would Plony Almony, who refused on the grounds that Ruth was a Moabite and hence forbidden. One answer given is that Boaz thought that [even if the halachic distinction of "a Moabite, not a Moabitess" is not invoked,] the positive precept of perpetuating a kinsman's name, by begetting progeny through his widow, i.e., *yibum*, displaced the negative precept forbidding marriage to a Moabite. Yet he feared that the seed from such a union would nonetheless be flawed. Therefore she said, "Spread your wing (cloak) over your handmaiden, for you are a redeemer." She urged him not to be concerned about her being a Moabite.

3:10 וַיֹּאמֶר בְּרוּכָה אַתְּ לַיהוָה בִּתִּי הֵיטַבְתְּ חַסְדֵּךְ הָאַחֲרוֹן מִן־הָרִאשׁוֹן לְבִלְתִּי־לֶכֶת אַחֲרֵי הַבַּחוּרִים אִם־דַּל וְאִם־עָשִׁיר:

He said, "Blessed are you of the Lord, my daughter! Your last kindness is greater than the first, by not going after the young men, whether poor or rich."

Ruth had feared that Boaz would curse her for approaching him at night on the threshing floor. But "one who trusts in the Lord is raised high" (Proverbs 29:25), and God inspired Boaz to bless her instead.

"Already you are blessed of God," he said, "included in the blessing of Abraham."

God had said to Abraham, "All the families of the earth will be blessed (ונברכו) through you" (Genesis 12:3), and our sages interpret ונברכו as "grafted," drawing upon the cognate מבריך. Thus the blessing is a reference to all righteous converts who would be "grafted" to the tree of Israel.

Similarly, Rabbi Dosa ben Harkinas said to Rabbi Akiba [who was descended from a family of converts], "Are you Akiba ben Joseph, whose name goes forth from one end of the earth to the other? May there be more [righteous converts] like you in Israel!"

Thus, although Ruth had called herself "your handmaiden," he replied that she was no less than "my daughter."

He praised her for making a habit of kindness, which began with providing shrouds for her husband; to wit, "May the Lord deal kindly with you as you have dealt with the deceased" (v. 1:8), embracing Judaism [which was a kindness to her soul], as it says, "be your reward complete from the Lord ... beneath Whose wings you have come to refuge" (v. 2:12), and in caring for the destitute Naomi—"It has been fully related to me all that you have done for your mother-in-law" (v. 2:11). But her latest act of kindness—seeking to marry the aged Boaz in order to perpetuate the name and soul of Machlon—surpassed all the rest. It was also מן הראשון, a result "of the first," for one good deed leads to another.

Boaz went on to praise her for not seeking to marry a younger man—perhaps even a relative of Elimelech—even though, as our sages observe, a woman generally prefers a poor young man to a rich old one. He also praised her for not having strayed after a rich man—in contrast to the general decadence and immorality of the generation.

There are three types of converts, say our sages. One converts to eat, and of him it is written, "To the convert in the gate shall you give it" (Deuteronomy 14:21). A second converts to receive charity, and of him it is written, "To the pauper and the convert shall you leave them" (Leviticus 19:10). The third converts for the sake of heaven. Of him the Torah says, "One statute for you and for the convert who dwells in your midst" (Numbers 15:15). By not going after the young men, Ruth proved that she had converted purely for the sake of heaven, and therefore was blessed of God, Who cherishes sincere converts.

3:11   וְעַתָּה בִּתִּי אַל־תִּירְאִי כֹּל אֲשֶׁר־תֹּאמְרִי אֶעֱשֶׂה־לָּךְ כִּי יוֹדֵעַ כָּל־שַׁעַר עַמִּי כִּי אֵשֶׁת חַיִל אָתְּ:

"And now, my daughter, fear not. All that you say I will do for you. For all the gate of my people know that a woman of valor are you."

"Fear not that I will turn you away because I am ashamed to marry a Moabite convert. On the contrary, all the people know that you are a righteous woman worthy of marrying the judge of Israel.

"Neither fear that you have blemished your reputation by coming here tonight, or that I will not force this matter to a swift conclusion. No one will condemn your action, for all know that you act solely for the sake of heaven."

In addition, Boaz assured her that she would be spared the usual suffering of converts, which occurs because they had delayed their conversion, or came out of fear rather than out of love for God, or are ignorant of the details of Jewish law. As everyone knew, Ruth hastened to convert out of love for God, and was strong in bearing the yoke of His laws.

Thus Boaz had earlier said to her, "be your reward complete from the Lord, God of Israel, beneath Whose wings you have come to shelter" (v. 2:12), adding now that she was "a woman of valor" in regard to keeping the commandments.

The term חַיִל, "valor" (numerical value 48) indicates that Boaz praised her for emulating Abraham, who abandoned idolatry at the age of forty-eight.

The numerical equivalent of חיל also hints at the forty-eight times proselytes are mentioned in the Torah.

He further praised her for being totally a woman of valor—hence אֵת, "from *aleph* (א) to *tav* (ת)."

Moreover, her being "a woman of valor" took her out of the category of "fatal wife," which designates a woman whose two successive husbands died [and whom one therefore should not marry]. That is, despite the fact that according to one opinion, Kilyon had married her by the law of levirate obligation (*yibum*) after the death of Machlon, and then he, too, died, she was not considered a "fatal wife."

3:12 וְעַתָּה כִּי אָמְנָם כִּי [אם] (כתיב ולא קרי) גֹאֵל אָנֹכִי וְגַם יֵשׁ גֹּאֵל קָרוֹב מִמֶּנִּי:

"Now while it is true that [if] I am a redeemer, there is also a redeemer closer than I."

The "redeemer" of whom Boaz spoke was Tov. According to our sages, Salmon [father of Boaz], Elimelech, and Tov were brothers. Tov, being a brother of Elimelech, was a closer relative than Boaz, who was only a nephew. According to others, Tov, Boaz, and Elimelech were brothers, which would mean that Tov must have been older than Boaz and hence took precedence.

Since the closer relative had to be given the option of redeeming Machlon's field, the outcome of the matter appeared to be uncertain, as reflected by the conditional אִם, "if." The text is read, however, כי גואל אנכי, "that I am a redeemer," without the word אִם, to hint that there was actually no uncertainty. Boaz would indeed be the one to redeem her.

3:13 לִינִי הַלַּיְלָה וְהָיָה בַבֹּקֶר אִם־יִגְאָלֵךְ טוֹב יִגְאָל וְאִם־לֹא יַחְפֹּץ לְגָאֳלֵךְ וּגְאַלְתִּיךְ אָנֹכִי חַי־יְהוָה שִׁכְבִי עַד־הַבֹּקֶר:

"Stay this night. And it shall be in the morning, if he will redeem you, good! let him redeem. But if he does not want to redeem you, I will redeem you. As the Lord lives! Lie until morning."

Presented with a plea for a kindness that was not in his power to grant immediately, the righteous Boaz reacted with characteristic consideration for the feelings of others. He at once assured Ruth that she was truly deserving of the kindness, and then apologized for not being able to fulfill her request immediately, explaining that it depended on another. Tov had to be offered the opportunity of redeeming her first.

He asked her to "stay the night" because it was unsafe for a woman to venture out alone at this late hour, and on the other hand harmful to their reputations for him to escort her.

But when Ruth, who had gone to Boaz thinking he would become her husband, heard that Tov might marry her instead, she rose to leave. Boaz therefore repeated his request that she "lie until morning."

She acquiesced and lay down, but her uncertainty about his response did not let her sleep. Was he trying to rebuff her with empty words? she wondered, perhaps aloud. Whereupon Boaz leaped up and swore ("As the Lord lives!") that he meant what he had said, and told her to sleep peacefully, confident that she would soon be redeemed.

Our sages say that his evil inclination tried to entice him, saying, "You are unmarried, and she is unmarried. . . ." Whereupon he swore to his evil inclination that he would not approach her except by marriage. He purified his thought to the point that he was willing to forgo his opportunity to redeem her in favor of Tov.

It is instructive in this regard to contrast the righteous judge of Israel with the degenerate Persian king Ahasuerus. When "the king's heart was glad with wine" he ordered his queen to appear dressed "in the royal crown"—and nothing else (Talmud)—"to show the peoples and the princes her beauty" (Esther 1:10,11). On the other hand, after Boaz "ate and drank and his heart was glad" (v. 7), and he found a beautiful woman, adorned, perfumed, and ritually pure from immersion, lying at his feet, he swore to his evil inclination that he would not touch her.

This righteous man's words, ליני הלילה, "stay this night," signify that only this night would Ruth stay alone, without a husband; the next morning she would be redeemed. Similarly, many generations later, the children of Israel would endure the night of exile, when they would be like a woman separated from her husband, with whom she will be reunited in the morning of her redemption. This is hinted at by ליני, which is composed of the end letters of the "four exiles"; Babylon (בב"ל), Media (מד"י), Greece (יו"ן), and Rome (רומ"י).

In this regard the letter *nun* (נ, numerically equivalent to 50), portends that the future exile would begin in the fiftieth generation, at the time of Nebuchadnezzar. Alternatively, the enlarged letter *nun* in certain texts alludes to the Messiah (a scion of Ruth), one of whose names was Yenon, יִנּוֹן. [Thus it says, "Yenon is his name" (Psalms 72:17).]

3:14 וַתִּשְׁכַּב מַרְגְּלוֹתָו עַד־הַבֹּקֶר וַתָּקָם בְּטֶרֶם יַכִּיר אִישׁ אֶת־רֵעֵהוּ וַיֹּאמֶר אַל־יִוָּדַע כִּי־בָאָה הָאִשָּׁה הַגֹּרֶן׃

She lay at his feet until the morning. Then she rose before a man could recognize his friend, for he said, "Let it not be known that the woman came to the threshing floor."

That night, while Ruth lay at the feet of Boaz, deep emotion over her future kept her awake.

Boaz, too, was awake. If her visit became public knowledge and a judge of Israel suspected of immoral conduct, it would be a desecration of God's name.

Our sages inform us that all night long he prostrated himself before God in prayer. "Master of the universe! It is revealed and known to You that I did not touch her. Let it then not become known that the woman came to the threshing floor, and let not the name of Heaven be desecrated through me."

Then at an hour when it is too dark to recognize even a close friend, Ruth rose at his request and made her exit.

His servants, too, were urged to secrecy; hence, "Let it not be known that the woman came!"

It is noteworthy that Boaz was careful about being in seclusion with a woman, although the prohibition of *yichud* as such was first enacted by David and his court three generations later.

In a different vein, following the farmers' custom of giving visitors to their fields some produce as a token gift, Boaz said, "Shall it not be known that the woman came to the threshing floor?" And he measured out for her six barley-corns, as described in the following verse.

3:15 וַיֹּאמֶר הָבִי הַמִּטְפַּחַת אֲשֶׁר־עָלַיִךְ וְאֶחֳזִי־בָהּ וַתֹּאחֶז בָּהּ וַיָּמָד שֵׁשׁ־שְׂעֹרִים וַיָּשֶׁת עָלֶיהָ וַיָּבֹא הָעִיר:

He said, "Bring the kerchief that is upon you and hold it." She held it, and he measured six barley-corns and set it upon her. Then he went into the city.

To keep her visit to the threshing floor secret, Boaz asked Ruth to remove her kerchief and to carry home a heavy load of grain, so that anyone seeing her leave would take her for a man returning from work with his pickings. As a further precaution, he addressed her in the masculine form (some texts have הבה rather than the feminine הבי) so that if his servants overheard, they would think he was speaking to one of the paupers. In addition, instead of having the servants bring a sack and measure the grain into it, he asked her to bring a kerchief, and measured out the grain himself.

To make the work easier for him, she "girded her loins with strength" like a man (Proverbs 31:17), that is, held all four corners herself, so that he had only to measure.

Or else, he did not ask her actually to remove her kerchief, but to grasp two ends of the triangle, into which he then poured the grain.

According to a different interpretation, Boaz and Ruth both grasped the kerchief as a contractual gesture—a sign that he undertook to settle her case. And he measured out a sixth (שֵׁשׁ) of a *seah*, that is, one *kab*—enough for one meal—to demonstrate that she would eat only one more meal at home before entering the home of her husband.

Now in *gematriya* הָבִי, "bring," has the value 17, and the last letters of המטפח״ת אש״ר עלי״ך, "the kerchief that is upon you," are those of כתר, crown, to hint that out of her would come seventeen generations of kings after the erection of the Temple.

According to our sages, he measured six grains of barley. That is, for every sixth of a *seah* that he measured out, he set aside one grain to keep count, and then gave her the six grains as a sign that he had measured six times.

The six grains were also a sign that from Ruth would descend six *tzaddikim*, each possessing six outstanding attributes: David, Chananiah, Mishael, Azariah, Daniel, and the Messiah. David, for example, is described as "skillful in playing, a mighty man of valor, a man of war, prudent in affairs, and comely of appearance, and the Lord is with him" (1 Samuel 16:18). Perhaps it is these six virtues that are represented by the six-pointed Shield of David (*magen david*, מָגֵן דָוִד).

3:16 וַתָּבוֹא אֶל־חֲמוֹתָהּ וַתֹּאמֶר מִי־אַתְּ בִּתִּי וַתַּגֶּד־לָהּ אֵת כָּל־אֲשֶׁר עָשָׂה־לָהּ הָאִישׁ:

She came to her mother-in-law, who said, "Who are you, my daughter?" So she told her all that the man had done for her.

Despite her heavy load, Ruth walked the long distance home with her characteristic quickness, and arrived while it was yet dark and the door was still locked. Her knock startled Naomi, who had just dozed off after a sleepless night of worry about Ruth. At the sight of a woman—concealed by a veil or perhaps by darkness—Naomi asked, "Who are you?"

She quickly recovered her presence of mind, however, and Ruth did not have to identify herself. Instead, she launched directly into an account of the night's events.

According to the Midrash, Naomi asked, "What is your situation? Are you despondent or hopeful? Are you single or married?" Ruth responded by recounting all that Boaz had done for her.

3:17 וַתֹּאמֶר שֵׁשׁ־הַשְּׂעֹרִים הָאֵלֶּה נָתַן לִי כִּי אָמַר אֵלַי (קרי ולא כתיב) אַל־תָּבוֹאִי רֵיקָם אֶל־חֲמוֹתֵךְ:

And she said, "These six barley-corns he gave me, for he said (to me), "Come not empty-handed to your mother-in-law."

Naomi might well have taken the grain as a sign that Boaz did not intend to redeem Ruth. For if she were about to enter his house, why was he sending provisions to *her* house? Therefore Ruth wisely added that the grain was for Naomi.

By sending Naomi a gift, she said, Boaz had indicated his wish that Ruth continue to remain close to her mother-in-law. In this way Ruth reassured Naomi that she would not forsake her after her marriage.

The term אֵלַי, "to me," though pronounced, is not written in the text, to hint at Ruth's hidden potential to become the forebear of the six righteous men (see earlier, on v. 15), symbolized by the six seedling grains.

3:18 וַתֹּאמֶר שְׁבִי בִתִּי עַד אֲשֶׁר תֵּדְעִין אֵיךְ יִפֹּל דָּבָר כִּי לֹא יִשְׁקֹט הָאִישׁ כִּי אִם־כִּלָּה הַדָּבָר הַיּוֹם:

Then she said, "Sit still, my daughter, until you know how the matter will fall. For the man will not rest unless he settles the matter today."

Ruth wanted to return to help with the winnowing, which could not possibly have been completed in a single evening. But Naomi advised her to stay home, in readiness for Boaz to call her. "It will not be long," she assured her. "Even as you are resting here, he will be busy settling the matter of your redemption."

Ruth worried that she might be redeemed by Tov, who had a wife and children, to which he later alluded when he said, "lest I ruin my inheritance" (v. 4:6). So Naomi told her to "sit." She could rest assured that Boaz would settle the matter, i.e., by redeeming her himself.

Naomi also prophesied that he had only "today" left to live.

RUTH 4

4:1 וּבֹעַז עָלָה הַשַּׁעַר וַיֵּשֶׁב שָׁם וְהִנֵּה הַגֹּאֵל עֹבֵר אֲשֶׁר דִּבֶּר־בֹּעַז וַיֹּאמֶר סוּרָה שְׁבָה־פֹּה פְּלֹנִי אַלְמֹנִי וַיָּסַר וַיֵּשֵׁב:

Meanwhile Boaz went up to the gate and sat down there. And behold! the redeemer was passing by, of whom Boaz had spoken. He said, "Turn aside, sit down here, so-and-so (Plony Almony)." So he turned aside and sat down.

Naomi was proven right in predicting that Boaz would not rest until Ruth was redeemed. Promptly, in the morning, he came directly "to the gate" [where matters of law were dealt with by the Sanhedrin], in order to fulfill his oath to Ruth.

He "went up." For as implied by Naomi's words earlier (v. 3:3), "Go down to the threshing ," the threshing floor was located in the lowest part of the city.

Despite his eagerness to settle the matter, however, he was determined to ensure the other redeemer a fair chance to exercise his right of redemption, and took pains to avoid giving the impression that he himself was determined to redeem Ruth. Boaz therefore did not go to the redeemer, but instead "sat down" in the gate (without first requesting permission, our sages note, for he was head of the Sanhedrin) and waited, as if to say, "I have done all I can. The rest is up to God." Perhaps he also prayed that the redeemer would come by. And indeed, no sooner had Boaz seated himself in the gate, then "behold! the redeemer was passing by," to fulfill the words that "Boaz had spoken" to Ruth: "And it shall be in the morning, if he will redeem you, let him redeem" (v. 3:13). Boaz had attained the degree of the most righteous, of whom the scripture says: "You will decree a thing, and it will be established for you" (Job 22:28).

"Behold! the redeemer was passing by." Was he standing behind the gate? asks the Midrash, and it answers: Even had he been at the other end of the world, God would have whisked him over so that the righteous Boaz would not have to wait.

The Midrash continues: Boaz did his part, Ruth and Naomi did theirs. And God said, "I, too, will do Mine." Immediately, He patterned events so that Boaz would wed Ruth, and thus the redeemer passed by within earshot so that Boaz could call him to "turn aside" (*surah*, סורה).

This unusual expression recalls Lot's invitation to the angels who had come to destroy Sodom—"Turn aside (*suru*, סורו) to the house of your servant" (Genesis 19:2). Intent upon saving Lot's family so that the mother of monarchy would come forth from them, they asked, "Who else have you here? A son-in-law, or sons...? Take them out of this place" (Genesis 19:12). But since the sons-in-law refused to flee, the spark of Ruth had to come instead through Lot himself.

Boaz now summoned the redeemer, addressing him by name, which the verse conceals to spare him embarrassment. According to the Midrash Tanchuma, his name was Tov, as it is written, "If Tov will redeem you (אם יגאלך טוב), let him redeem" (v. 3:13). However, according to the Ibn Ezra interpretation that *tov* (טוב) is the common noun meaning good or fine—"If he will redeem you, good! let him redeem"—the scripture never reveals his name.

Because he did not want to redeem Ruth, he is called simply פלוני אלמוני (*plony almony*), "so-and-so"—a nonentity. *Almony* means nameless, as in אלמנה (*almana*), a widow, who does not bear the name of a husband; and as in אִלֵם (*ilem*), mute, for his name is not pronounced.

In addition, the redeemer was "mute" in matters of halacha, for he did not know that a female Moabite convert is permitted to marry a Jew.

According to a different interpretation, Boaz said to the redeemer, "Although you are *plony almony*, a retiring person who seeks anonymity, the time demands that you turn aside from your usual modesty, and seat yourself here in the gate."

Plony almony also means hidden and secret: the fact that he was being offered the opportunity of establishing the kingdom was hidden from him. This is evident from his refusal to redeem Ruth "lest I ruin my inheritance" (v. 6), which Boaz took as a sign that Ruth was divinely designated for himself.

4:2 וַיִּקַּח עֲשָׂרָה אֲנָשִׁים מִזִּקְנֵי הָעִיר וַיֹּאמֶר שְׁבוּ־פֹה וַיֵּשֵׁבוּ:

He then took ten men of the city's elders and said, "Sit here," and they sat down.

To publicize the halacha permitting a Moabite woman to convert and marry a Jew, Boaz assembled ten elders. They would also serve as the necessary quorum for the marriage ceremony about to take place, and safeguard modesty and propriety at the wedding festivities, as was customary. Possibly the members of the Sanhedrin were not present, since Boaz, its head, had gone directly from the threshing floor to the gate without stopping to summon them.

But even if the judges of the Sanhedrin were present, Boaz nevertheless "took ten men" in order to highlight the specific halacha that a marriage must take place in the presence of a quorum of ten. Furthermore, he did not want to appear before the court which he headed as a litigant defending his own interest. And in order not to disturb the proceedings of the Sanhedrin, he "took" those ten men off to the side and asked them to "sit." They promptly complied out of respect for Boaz.

According to a different interpretation, he gave them permission to be seated, from which our sages infer that one may not sit in the presence of a greater man without the latter's permission.

The Marriage Blessings

Contracting a marriage originally was carried out in two stages, which were set apart from each other by as much as a year. The first stage was the *erusin* or *kiddushin* (betrothal) ceremony, which today consists of the groom giving the bride a ring. The second stage was the *nesuin* or marriage, where the bride and groom symbolically began their life together as husband and wife in the nuptial ceremony under the *chupah* (marriage canopy, representing a house).

Eventually, to avoid complications, our sages instituted the practice of holding both ceremonies together; and *kiddushin*, too, takes place today under the *chupah*.

The word *erusin* (ארוסין) stems from the verb *aras* (ארס), which is closely related to the word *asar* (אסר), to bind. *Kiddushin* (קדושין) means sanctification or consecration, literally setting apart—reserving the particular woman for the particular man. The second stage of the marriage is called *nesuin* (נשואין), which is derived from the verb *nasa* (נשא), to take. A man takes a woman in marriage.

The Blessings of Kiddushin

The man who betroths a woman must pronounce a blessing prior to the performance of this mitzvah. This Prenuptial Blessing (*Birkath Erusin,* ברכת ארוסין) is:

בָּרוּךְ אַתָּה יְיָ אֱלֹהֵינוּ מֶלֶךְ הָעוֹלָם אֲשֶׁר קִדְּשָׁנוּ בְּמִצְוֹתָיו, וְצִוָּנוּ עַל הָעֲרָיוֹת, וְאָסַר לָנוּ אֶת הָאֲרוּסוֹת, וְהִתִּיר לָנוּ אֶת הַנְּשׂוּאוֹת לָנוּ עַל יְדֵי חֻפָּה וְקִדּוּשִׁין. בָּרוּךְ אַתָּה יְיָ, מְקַדֵּשׁ עַמּוֹ יִשְׂרָאֵל עַל יְדֵי חֻפָּה וְקִדּוּשִׁין:

Blessed are You, O Lord our God, King of the universe, who sanctified us with His commandments, and commanded us concerning sexual prohibitions, forbidding to us [women] who are [merely] betrothed, but permitting to us [women] who are wed to us through chupah *and* kiddushin. *Blessed are You, O Lord, who sanctifies Israel through* chupah *and* kiddushin.

The Rambam writes that the groom pronounces the blessing. However, it is customary for another to recite it for him, so as not to embarrass a groom who may not know how to recite it. This is similar to the practice instituted for the reading of the Torah in the synagogue.

The blessing is recited over a cup of wine. If there is no wine, the blessing is recited without it. The groom and bride are given to sip, and the one who pronounced the blessing has thereby discharged his obligation to drink after reciting the blessing over wine. This is similar to the halacha for *Kiddush* and *Havdalah,* where one exempts the other for the blessing over wine.

בָּרוּךְ אַתָּה יְהֹוָה אֱלֹהֵינוּ מֶלֶךְ הָעוֹלָם, בּוֹרֵא פְּרִי הַגָּפֶן:

Blessed are You, O Lord our God, King of the universe, Who creates the fruit of the grapevine.

The blessing over *kiddushin* requires a quorum of ten men, including the groom. Relatives as well may be counted toward the ten. But if there is no quorum, it may be recited nevertheless.

If one did not pronounce the blessing of *kiddushin* at the time the *kiddushin* is performed, according to some authorities he recites it together with the blessing of *nesuin* under the *chupah*. Others say that he should then consecrate her a second time beneath the *chupah* so that the blessing will be close to the consecration.

The Blessings of Nesuin

Today the custom is to perform the *kiddushin* as well under the *chupah*, and since blessings over wine are recited for both *kiddushin* and *nesuin*, two cups of wine are required. The blessing "Who creates the fruit of the grapevine" is recited over each cup separately. However, an interval of time should be allowed between the first cup, over which the groom consecrates the bride, and the second cup.

The blessings of *nesuin* cannot be recited by the groom, since they are meant to bless the couple with success. The custom is that the bride and groom stand facing east, and the one pronouncing the blessings faces them, just as for the Priestly Blessings.

Although all blessings are recited before the event for which it is required, the custom is to recite the blessings of *kiddushin* and *nesuin* under the *chupah* because they are a prayer.

The blessings of *nesuin* are recited in the presence of ten adult males, including the groom, since they are blessings of joy and the groom is joyous. This applies when they are recited under the *chupah* or during the meal.

בָּרוּךְ אַתָּה יְהֹוָה אֱלֹהֵינוּ מֶלֶךְ הָעוֹלָם, שֶׁהַכֹּל בָּרָא לִכְבוֹדוֹ:

1. Blessed are You, O Lord our God, King of the universe, who created all things for His glory.

בָּרוּךְ אַתָּה יְהֹוָה אֱלֹהֵינוּ מֶלֶךְ הָעוֹלָם, יוֹצֵר הָאָדָם:

2. Blessed are You, O Lord our God, King of the universe, Creator of man.

בָּרוּךְ אַתָּה יְהֹוָה אֱלֹהֵינוּ מֶלֶךְ הָעוֹלָם, אֲשֶׁר יָצַר אֶת הָאָדָם בְּצַלְמוֹ, בְּצֶלֶם דְּמוּת תַּבְנִיתוֹ, וְהִתְקִין לוֹ מִמֶּנּוּ בִּנְיַן עֲדֵי עַד. בָּרוּךְ אַתָּה יְהֹוָה, יוֹצֵר הָאָדָם:

3. Blessed are You, O Lord our God, King of the universe, who created man in His image, in the image set

forth by his structure, and who prepared for him from him a structure to last for all time. Blessed are You, O Lord, Creator of man.

שׂוֹשׂ תָּשִׂישׂ וְתָגֵל הָעֲקָרָה, בְּקִבּוּץ בָּנֶיהָ לְתוֹכָהּ בְּשִׂמְחָה. בָּרוּךְ אַתָּה יְהוָֹה, מְשַׂמֵּחַ צִיּוֹן בְּבָנֶיהָ:

4. May she who is barren rejoice and exult, when her children are gathered within her in joy. Blessed are You, O Lord, who makes Zion rejoice in her children.

שַׂמֵּחַ תְּשַׂמַּח רֵעִים הָאֲהוּבִים, כְּשַׂמֵּחֲךָ יְצִירְךָ בְּגַן עֵדֶן מִקֶּדֶם. בָּרוּךְ אַתָּה יְהוָֹה, מְשַׂמֵּחַ חָתָן וְכַלָּה:

5. Grant joy to these loving companions, even as You gladdened long ago Your creature in the Garden of Eden. Blessed are You, O Lord, who grants joy to bridegroom and bride.

בָּרוּךְ אַתָּה יְהוָֹה אֱלֹהֵינוּ מֶלֶךְ הָעוֹלָם, אֲשֶׁר בָּרָא שָׂשׂוֹן וְשִׂמְחָה, חָתָן וְכַלָּה, גִּילָה רִנָּה, דִּיצָה וְחֶדְוָה, אַהֲבָה וְאַחֲוָה, וְשָׁלוֹם וְרֵעוּת, מְהֵרָה יְהוָֹה אֱלֹהֵינוּ יִשָּׁמַע בְּעָרֵי יְהוּדָה וּבְחוּצוֹת יְרוּשָׁלַיִם, קוֹל שָׂשׂוֹן, וְקוֹל שִׂמְחָה, קוֹל חָתָן וְקוֹל כַּלָּה, קוֹל מִצְהֲלוֹת חֲתָנִים מֵחֻפָּתָם, וּנְעָרִים מִמִּשְׁתֵּה נְגִינָתָם. בָּרוּךְ אַתָּה יְהוָֹה, מְשַׂמֵּחַ חָתָן עִם הַכַּלָּה:

6. Blessed are You, O Lord our God, King of the universe, who created joy and gladness, bridegroom and bride, rejoicing and song, cheer and delight, love and harmony, peace and fellowship. Soon, O Lord our God, may there be heard in the cities of Judah and in the streets of Jerusalem, a voice of joy and gladness, the voice of the bridegroom and the voice of the bride, the jubilant voices of bridegrooms from their wedding canopies, and of youths from their feasts of song. Blessed are You, O Lord, who grants joy to the bridegroom with the bride.

Since "Who created all things for His Glory" is said in honor of the assembled guests, and the rebuilding of Jerusalem is mentioned, it is not proper to recite the Seven Blessings if there are less than a quorum of ten. This is inferred from Boaz. [Even though Boaz assembled ten men besides himself,] the groom is counted toward the ten. On the other days of post-nuptial feasting, therefore, if there are no "new faces" (see below) among the guests and only "who created . . . joy" is recited, a quorum of ten is not required. Three men are needed, however, to satisfy the minimum requirement of *Zimun* for the Grace after Meals.

Some say that if in a particular place it is impossible to assemble ten men, one is not to marry there, but must seek out a place where a quorum can be had. Many are of the opinion, however, that in such a case the wedding should be held anyway, and the blessings recited a number of days earlier. But the blessing "Who has created" should be recited at the meal.

Others say that the Seven Blessings should not be postponed beyond the seven days of post-nuptial celebration.

If the ceremony was begun with ten people present, but some left, there are authorities who allow the ceremony to be completed, as in the case of saying *"Borchu!"* and of *Kaddish*.

It is customary under the *chupah* to recite the blessing over wine before the other blessings, and at the meal it is recited after the Grace. The reason is that the blessing over wine is frequent and fixed (*tadir*, תדיר)—as at *Kiddush* every Sabbath Eve—while the others are occasional, and a practice that is *tadir* takes precedence. On the other hand, at the meal it comes last, to make it evident that the cup of wine pertains to the other blessings.

Explanation of the Blessings

1. The first blessing, "Who created all things for His glory," is not part of the order, but is in honor of the assembled multitudes who gathered as an act of lovingkindness (*chesed*, חסד) for the bride and groom. It commemorates all the *chesed* that God lavished upon the first man. Since there is a blessing over wine, it was arranged with all these blessings (Rashi, Kethuboth 8).

Because it is an independent blessing and not part of the order, it opens with *"Baruch"* although it is adjacent to the blessing over wine. Moreover, at the meal it is the first blessing, hence it must begin with *"Baruch."* Another reason is that it is a brief blessing, and if it did not begin with *"Baruch"* it would not be evident that it is a blessing.

2. "Creator of man" is the first blessing of the order. [And man has so been created to require a wife, as it is written, "It is not good for a man to be alone" (Genesis 2:18).]

3. The matter of marriage is begun in this second blessing of the order. "Who created man in His image" refers to the male, and "prepared for him from him a structure to last for all time" refers to the female [who bears future generations and maintains the home].

4. "Rejoice and exult" is said because we are obligated to set Jerusalem above our greatest joy, as it is written, "Let my tongue cleave to my palate . . . if I do not raise Jerusalem above my chief joy" (Psalms 138:6).

5. "Grant joy" is a blessing to the bride and groom for happiness and well-being. These "loving companions" should know gladness such as that which God granted to the first man long ago in the Garden of Eden.

6. This blessing concludes with the words, "Who grants joy to the bridegroom with the bride," whereas the previous blessing concluded with "Who grants joy to the bridegroom *and* bride." For that was a blessing for their success in life, a prayer for material plenty and well-being, while the present blessing gives praise to God for having created weddings and the cleaving of a husband to his wife through gladness and delight. And "Who grants joy to the bridegroom with the bride" thus gives expression to this delight of the husband with the wife.

In some places it is customary that a myrtle is brought to the *chupah*, and a blessing recited over it after the blessing on the wine. Then the other six blessings are recited (Rambam).

Where no wine is available, one should soak raisins in water, squeeze them out, and recite the blessing over it. If there are no raisins either, any "beer-like" beverage can be used and the "Shehakol" recited over it. If no cup at all can be had, the *nesuin* ceremony cannot proceed.

For the *erusin* blessings, on the other hand, if no cup is available, the *erusin* blessing ("Who has sanctified us . . .") alone is said. According to some authorities, also for the *erusin* if no wine is available one makes the blessing over beer (Ramban, Tur).

The reason that the cup is crucial to the blessing of the *erusin* ceremony is that there must be seven blessings, just as there are seven days of feasting, and one of the seven is the blessing over wine.

There are seven days of blessing for a virgin and only one for a widow. For a virgin all seven blessings are recited after the meal, following the Grace after Meals.

For a widow none of these blessings is ever recited on the second and third day, not even "Who created." The only blessing recited is at the *Zimun* preceding the Grace after Meals:

בָּרוּךְ אֱלֹהֵינוּ שֶׁהַשִּׂמְחָה בִּמְעוֹנוֹ וְשֶׁאָכַלְנוּ מִשֶּׁלּוֹ וּבְטוּבוֹ חָיִינוּ:

Blessed be our God, in whose domain is joy, whose food we have eaten, and through whose goodness we live.

A "New Face"

When there is a "new face" (*panim chadashoth*, פנים חדשות) among the celebrants at the feast, all seven blessings are recited; if not, only *Asher bara* ("Who created"). In the view of some, even that is recited only if others participate in the Grace after Meals.

Rambam writes that a "new face" includes one who has not heard the Seven Blessings recited. Most authorities, however, define a "new face" as one who has not yet partaken of any of the festive meals.

Some include only men of stature for whom it is fitting that food be added to the meal. Others consider a "new face" to include even those who do not partake of the meal, and all Seven Blessings are recited in their presence.

If the day of the feast is itself distinguished—a Sabbath or a holiday—that is considered a "new face." According to some, this holds true only for the morning or evening meal, not for the third meal [on the Sabbath]. However, it has now become customary to recite the blessings also at the third meal—some say because it is customary to deliver a Torah discourse at this time.

4:3 וַיֹּאמֶר לַגֹּאֵל חֶלְקַת הַשָּׂדֶה אֲשֶׁר לְאָחִינוּ לֶאֱלִימֶלֶךְ מָכְרָה נָעֳמִי הַשָּׁבָה מִשְּׂדֵה מוֹאָב:

Then he said to the redeemer, "The portion of field that was our brother Elimelech's has Naomi sold, who returned from the Fields of Moab."

Boaz urged the redeemer to fulfill his obligation of redeeming the field, in accordance with the Torah law: "If your brother becomes impoverished and sells of his possessions, the redeemer who is close to him will come and redeem that which his brother has sold" (Leviticus 25:25).

"Now the righteous Naomi (she whose deeds are pleasing)," said Boaz, "is selling Elimelech's field, not out of disregard for her husband's inheritance but because she has returned from Moab impoverished and needs to sustain herself. Purchase therefore the field of our brother Elimelech, who was a great man, so that his name will not be forgotten and his ancestral inheritance will not fall into a stranger's hands.

"This field is part of a larger one left by their father to be divided among Elimelech, Tov, and Salmon; and it is unfitting for a stranger to intrude."

Since a field may not be redeemed until two years after it is sold, Naomi must have sold hers while she was still in Moab. Or else, the sale took place after her return three months earlier, but since the seller was not the owner but his widow [who only "owned" the field in the sense that she had the right to collect her marriage settlement from it], the field could be redeemed immediately.

That is, according to Torah law the two-year moratorium protects the rights of the buyer only if the field is sold directly by the owner, not if sold by court order for sustenance, as in Naomi's case.

4:4 וַאֲנִי אָמַרְתִּי אֶגְלֶה אָזְנְךָ לֵאמֹר קְנֵה נֶגֶד הַיֹּשְׁבִים וְנֶגֶד זִקְנֵי עַמִּי אִם־תִּגְאַל גְּאָל וְאִם־לֹא יִגְאַל הַגִּידָה לִּי וְאֵדְעָ[ה] כִּי אֵין זוּלָתְךָ לִגְאוֹל וְאָנֹכִי אַחֲרֶיךָ וַיֹּאמֶר אָנֹכִי אֶגְאָל:

"And I thought I would disclose it to you, saying: 'Buy it before those sitting here, and before the elders of my people. If you will redeem, redeem! And if he will not redeem, tell me, that I may know. For there is none to redeem besides you, and I after you.'"

And he said, "I will redeem."

When the people saw the elders sitting in the gate, they, too, assembled and were "sitting there." And before the large gathering, Boaz declared that he had made no attempt to acquire the field for himself, but as soon as he became aware of the situation, his first action was to "disclose it to you." He thought it within the redeemer's right to buy the field; moreover, since Ruth was so evidently a woman of valor, he had no reason to think the other would refuse on account of her.

Boaz thus made it clear that he himself was impartial in this matter, and the redeemer's choice was in no way compromised by the present facts.

Boaz began by telling the redeemer to "buy" the field; but that was only "before the elders," i.e., in keeping with the accepted norm that a buyer will try to lower the price by disparaging the merchandise. On the other hand, a redeemer who cherishes his ancestral inheritance will willingly pay more than its value. And therefore Boaz added that he was really asking him to "redeem" the field and pay the higher price.

The verse switches from the second person (*tigal*, תִּגְאַל) to the third (*yigal*, יִגְאַל). That is, "If you will redeem, redeem!" was said by Boaz; and "If he will not redeem, tell me, that I may know," was said by one of the elders, or else by Boaz addressing the elders.

According to a different interpretation, יִגְאַל, *yigal*, here does not mean "he will redeem," but is the redeemer's name. Boaz said to the redeemer: "If [it is] not [to be] Yigal, let me know!"

Or else, Boaz uses the third person in addressing the redeemer in order not to embarrass him. When speaking of fulfilling a *mitzvah* and redeeming the field, Boaz addressed him directly: "If you will redeem, redeem!" But when it came to refusing, he said tactfully in the third person "If he will not redeem. . . ."

He insisted upon a definite answer, so if the redeemer would not redeem, Boaz would.

4:5 וַיֹּאמֶר בֹּעַז בְּיוֹם־קְנוֹתְךָ הַשָּׂדֶה מִיַּד נָעֳמִי וּמֵאֵת רוּת הַמּוֹאֲבִיָּה אֵשֶׁת־הַמֵּת קָנִיתָ לְהָקִים שֵׁם־הַמֵּת עַל־נַחֲלָתוֹ׃

Then Boaz said, "The day you buy the field from the hand of Naomi, from Ruth the Moabite, the wife of the deceased, have you also bought it, to raise up the name of the deceased on his inheritance."

At first Boaz had spoken only of purchasing the field from Naomi, for if the redeemer refused, there was no point in embarrassing Ruth by mentioning her. Once however the redeemer agreed to buy the field,

Boaz added that although Naomi had the major "hand" in it, the field could not be bought without Ruth's consent—and Ruth refused to sell unless the buyer married her.

"Do not think it is sufficient to take Ruth into your house and support her," said Boaz. "The day you buy the field from Naomi, you must take Ruth as your wife to beget from her an heir for Elimelech. The child will inherit Elimelech's field, and the name of the deceased will be perpetuated on his earthly inheritance."

In another sense, producing offspring for the deceased would also bring rest to his soul in the World to Come, provided that the intention of the marriage partners was purely "to raise up the name of the deceased on his inheritance," as in *yibum*. A man who feels incapable of such pure intention must decline to perform the *mitzvah* of *yibum*, for the Zohar says that any personal attraction between the two parties in *yibum* prevents the redemption of the deceased. Boaz thus hinted that the redeemer should not wed Ruth unless he could do so with the pure intent of redeeming the deceased.

4:6 וַיֹּאמֶר הַגֹּאֵל לֹא אוּכַל לִגְאָל־לִי פֶּן־אַשְׁחִית אֶת־נַחֲלָתִי גְּאַל־לְךָ אַתָּה אֶת־גְּאֻלָּתִי כִּי לֹא־אוּכַל לִגְאֹל׃

The redeemer said, "I cannot redeem for myself, lest I ruin my inheritance. Redeem my redemption for yourself, for I cannot redeem."

Upon hearing that the redemption of which Boaz spoke meant acquiring not only Elimelech's field but also Machlon's wife, the redeemer retracted his original decision. "I cannot redeem the woman," he said, "lest I ruin my inheritance. Therefore I cannot redeem the field either."

By "inheritance" he was also referring to his first wife—as the scripture says, "House and wealth are an inheritance from fathers, but from the Lord is an intelligent wife" (Proverbs 19:14). The redeemer feared that having two wives in his home would ruin his marital harmony, and suggested that Boaz, a widower, undertake to redeem Ruth instead.

Since the stated purpose of the marriage was "to raise up a name for the deceased," he objected that "I cannot redeem *for myself*," i.e., the offspring would not be considered his own. Furthermore, he felt incapable of directing his thoughts solely to that selfless purpose, and feared that the levirate marriage would be to him a stumbling block to sin. For *yibum* is akin to incest if performed with any intention other than perpetuating the name of the deceased.

Accordingly, he said, "Take my obligation of redemption upon yourself." The aged Boaz, having mastered his evil inclination, could wed Ruth with the pure intention of perpetuating Machlon's name.

The redeemer was also wary of marrying a Moabite. For while Boaz held that a Moabitess was permitted to enter the congregation of God, he disagreed. According to our sages, that is one reason he was called Plony Almony (פְּלֹנִי אַלְמֹנִי)—he was mute (*ilem*, אִלֵּם) in halachic matters.

He was afraid for himself: Her first husband died because he had married her—should he do the same? In addition, he was afraid of bringing stigma and suffering upon his descendants, his "inheritance," as it is written, "Children are an inheritance from the Lord" (Psalms 127:3). He therefore said two times "I cannot redeem"—once for his own sake and once for the sake of his children.

It is, however, puzzling that the redeemer was not aware of the recently clarified halacha that Moabite women converts are permitted to marry Jews. Moreover, the entire Sanhedrin (according to one interpretation) had heard Boaz ask him to marry Ruth "the Moabitess" and had raised no objection. And if the redeemer thought it was forbidden, he would not have dared tell Boaz to "take my obligation [of redemption] for yourself."

Possibly the redeemer felt that it was not for a common man like himself to marry a Moabitess, lest the ruling later be contested, and he and his descendants be cut off from society. Only a leader of Israel could set the precedent and thereby make the halacha of "a Moabite, not a Moabitess" known throughout Israel.

[His fears, it later turned out, were justified. As already noted, the Talmud relates that when King Saul investigated the lineage of the young shepherd David to ascertain whether he was of royal stock (1 Samuel 17:58), Doeg the Edomite, head of the Sanhedrin and adviser to the king, stepped forward and said: "Instead of asking whether or not he is worthy of kingship, ask whether or not he is fit to enter the congregation of God! He is descended from Ruth the Moabite." With this he touched off a violent controversy.]

The redeemer had, however, a more prosaic objection to redeeming Elimelech's field. The large outlay of money would leave him short of

Ruth 4

funds with which to hire workers to cultivate his own field, and "my inheritance" would fall into ruin from neglect.

When Boaz heard the redeemer turn down the opportunity of establishing the royal dynasty "lest I ruin my inheritance," he understood that God had ordained Ruth as a wife for himself.

4:7 וְזֹאת לְפָנִים בְּיִשְׂרָאֵל עַל־הַגְּאוּלָּה וְעַל־הַתְּמוּרָה לְקַיֵּם כָּל־דָּבָר שָׁלַף אִישׁ נַעֲלוֹ וְנָתַן לְרֵעֵהוּ וְזֹאת הַתְּעוּדָה בְּיִשְׂרָאֵל:

Now this was [done] in former times in Israel concerning redemption and concerning exchange, to confirm every matter: a man drew off his shoe and gave it to his neighbor. This was the attestation in Israel.

Before describing the ceremony of "removing the shoe" (*chalitzah*, חליצה) that now took place, the scripture explains that it was an early custom in Israel which attained the force of Torah law, in accordance with the principle that "a custom of Israel is Torah" (Talmud).

The custom under discussion is the practice that in the sale ("redemption") or barter ("exchange") of an item, the seller removed his shoe and gave it to the buyer to symbolize the transfer of goods. Or, according to a different interpretation, the buyer gave the seller his shoe to symbolize his willingness to pay, even if it meant taking the very shirt off his back (or shoe off his foot).

Beyond its symbolism, the act had legal force: with it the transaction took effect. Hence "this was the attestation in Israel"—this was the act that witnesses observed and to which they testified in order to confirm the transaction.

Accordingly, after the ceremony Boaz said to those present: "Witnesses are you this day that I have purchased all that is Elimelech's" (v. 9).

A different interpretation is that formerly in Israel the practice was לקיים כל דבר, "to confirm every utterance"; a verbal agreement sufficed to confirm any transaction. Later it became customary to hand over the shoe as an act of acquisition, but it was done privately. "This was the attestation in Israel"; witnesses were not needed.

However, Plony Almony, being ignorant of Torah law, told Boaz *before the elders* to "buy it for yourself" (v. 8), that is, make an acquisition before witnesses. And Boaz acquiesced.

Another interpretation is that at first it was customary to remove the shoe for purchase ("redemption"); for barter ("exchange"), a more rare transaction, the practice was added later. Eventually it was used "to confirm every matter."

The exception was in acquiring a wife, because the shoe obviously had to be returned to the owner so he would not be left barefoot. If however the bride returned the shoe [it might appear as if she had rejected the act of betrothal], and hence it would seem that they lived together thereafter without benefit of proper wedlock. Thus it is an explicit halacha that a woman may not be wedded with a conditional gift, that is, one meant to be returned.

Accordingly, the marriage of Ruth and Boaz is described separately (v. 10); the shoe removal ceremony was only for acquiring the field.

Yet another interpretation is that handing over a shoe was done to "redeem" the wife of the deceased, and to "exchange" one redeemer for another if the latter, like Plony Almony, refused to redeem.

Similar use of a shoe is found in the Torah law of *chalitzah*, marking the refusal to perform *yibum*. We find also that when Joab took Abner aside "to speak to him privately (בַּשֶּׁלִי)" (2 Samuel 3:27), he was as if offering him entry into a covenant with the removal of a shoe (as in של נעלך, "Remove your shoe" [Joshua 5:15]).

However, the Targum translates נַעַל as "glove" rather than shoe. Nowadays, in the similar custom, commonly called *kinyan challipin* or simply *challipin*, the shoe is replaced by a handkerchief; and the transaction is known as a *kinyan sudar* (קִנְיָן סוּדָר, "acquisition by kerchief").

The Zohar says that here handing over a shoe is specified; it was a forgotten custom which Boaz now reinstituted. The scripture attests to its authenticity by recording that "This was the attestation in Israel."

Acquisition through *challipin* was one of two halachot that Boaz reinstituted that day, the other being that a Moabitess convert may enter the congregation of God.

Ordinarily, if a Torah scholar expounds a hitherto unknown halacha before the fact—i.e., before the situation to which his ruling applies has risen—he is believed; after the fact, he is not. But if he expounds two such halachot, it is a sign that they were based on a reliable tradition, and he is believed concerning both. Now that Ruth was about to marry a Jew

Ruth 4

(or: had already earlier married Machlon), the halacha of "a Moabite, not a Moabitess" was considered as coming after the fact. However, since Boaz simultaneously renewed the law of *challipin*, which "was done in former times in Israel," he was believed as well about "a Moabite, not a Moabitess."

4:8 וַיֹּאמֶר הַגֹּאֵל לְבֹעַז קְנֵה־לָךְ וַיִּשְׁלֹף נַעֲלוֹ׃

The redeemer said to Boaz, "Buy it for yourself," and he drew off his shoe.

In the manner of acquisition by *challipin*, Boaz removed his shoe and gave it to the redeemer in exchange for the right of redemption. This entitled Boaz to buy the field from Naomi and then acquire Ruth in a separate transaction.

According to a different interpretation, the redeemer passed his shoe to Boaz, as if to say, "Just as I have given you my shoe, so have I given you the right of redemption." Thus the following verse begins with "Boaz said," suggesting that "he drew off his shoe" is not speaking of Boaz.

4:9 וַיֹּאמֶר בֹּעַז לַזְּקֵנִים וְכָל־הָעָם עֵדִים אַתֶּם הַיּוֹם כִּי קָנִיתִי אֶת־כָּל־אֲשֶׁר לֶאֱלִימֶלֶךְ וְאֵת כָּל־אֲשֶׁר לְכִלְיוֹן וּמַחְלוֹן מִיַּד נָעֳמִי׃

Then Boaz said to the elders and to all the people: "Witnesses are you this day that I have purchased all that is Elimelech's and all that is Kilyon's and Machlon's from the hand of Naomi."

After the redeemer renounced his right of redemption, Boaz appointed witnesses for the purchase of the field. Before their eyes, he removed his shoe and purchased all the property of Elimelech and his sons by a *kinyan sudar* (see v. 7) "from the hand of Naomi." This may also mean that Naomi was present.

Also present was a large crowd, who had gathered to learn the word of God and His laws from the elders in the gate. This had been the practice ever since "the people stood on Moses from the morning to the evening" (Exodus 18:13) "because the people came to me to seek God" (Exodus 18:16). It was an occasion for Boaz to disseminate the halacha of "a Moabite, not a Moabitess," and thus make it clear that the elders fully concurred to his marrying Ruth.

Moreover, Boaz chose to make the purchase before a large crowd so that anyone who had a claim to the field would come forward. For Naomi might possibly have sold her field to someone else before departing for the Fields of Moab. Although two witnesses are sufficient to confirm a sale, he designated them all as witnesses, for a claimant who previously signs as a witness forfeits his claim. Thus he ensured that his purchase could not be contested later.

In accordance with the law that a deed dated before or after a sale takes place is invalid, Boaz stressed that they were witnesses "this day."

Thereby he accented that he had not acquired the field previously, but had given the redeemer his rightful chance to redeem. Only "this day," after the redeemer refused, did Boaz buy the field.

He also urged them to complete the matter quickly, and not postpone it till the next day.

Thus Boaz now acquired all of Elimelech's property which had been inherited by his sons, as well as the sons' property, which upon their death had reverted to Elimelech's estate. However, since Naomi had a lien on Elimelech's property to pay her marriage settlement (*kethubah*), and Ruth had a similar lien on the brothers' property, which she had given Naomi as a gift, Boaz purchased all the property of Elimelech and his sons "from the hand of Naomi."

According to a different interpretation, Boaz acquired everything of Kilyon's and Machlon's that had come to Ruth from the hand of Naomi. That is, when Kilyon and Machlon were about to wed the daughters of Eglon, a king, the widowed Naomi had made them wealthy by giving them property to which her *kethubah* entitled her. Ruth had returned this property to Naomi, from whom Boaz now bought it.

Still another interpretation is that Boaz acquired "all that is Elimelech's," that is, not only that part of the field being sold by Naomi, on which she had a lien for her marriage settlement and which she was now selling, but also the rest of his field, and other fields of Elimelech that Machlon and Kilyon had inherited. In addition, Boaz bought all that Machlon and Kilyon had acquired on their own, which was to be divided equally among Naomi and Elimelech's brothers, Salmon and Tov. Tov had now relinquished his share, and Salmon's portion was bought by his son Boaz, so that when Naomi sold Boaz her portion, Boaz acquired the *entire* property "from the hand of Naomi"—through her.

"From the hand of Naomi" may also allude to property which she had bought as a dowry to Elimelech. This she now sold to Boaz.

Although Ruth's husband Machlon, the older and greater of the two brothers, is usually mentioned before Kilyon, here the order is reversed to reflect the order of death, if Kilyon had died first, or the order of inheritance, if Machlon had died first. [In the latter case, Boaz would thus have said in effect, "I have bought not only Kilyon's property, but also that of Machlon, who died earlier."]

If it was actually Machlon who had died first, not only had Kilyon inherited his property, but he may have also taken Ruth in levirate marriage (see earlier). The following verse nonetheless refers to her as the "wife of Machlon," for Kilyon had only married her on account of Machlon.

4:10 וְגַם אֶת־רוּת הַמֹּאֲבִיָּה אֵשֶׁת מַחְלוֹן קָנִיתִי לִי לְאִשָּׁה לְהָקִים שֵׁם־הַמֵּת עַל־נַחֲלָתוֹ וְלֹא־יִכָּרֵת שֵׁם־הַמֵּת מֵעִם אֶחָיו וּמִשַּׁעַר מְקוֹמוֹ עֵדִים אַתֶּם הַיּוֹם:

"Also Ruth the Moabite, wife of Machlon, have I acquired for myself as a wife, to raise up the name of the dead upon his inheritance, that the name of the dead be not cut off from among his brothers and from the gate of his place. Witnesses are you this day."

After the redemption of the field was completed, Ruth was brought, and the marriage ceremony took place in the presence of the Sanhedrin ("the gate of his place") and the assembled multitude, whom he appointed witnesses, so that it would be well remembered that the wedding of Ruth "the Moabite" was celebrated with great publicity and with the approval of the Sanhedrin. No later *Beth Din* would then contest what had been sanctioned by this *Beth Din*.

For the same reason, Boaz said he had "acquired" Ruth, to convey that the marriage was legal and binding, for the ruling of "a Moabite, not a Moabitess" had been promulgated just before "this day." She could not otherwise have been consecrated to him in marriage, for consecration (*kiddushin*, קידושין) does not apply in regard to a gentile.

The "Moabite" (lit. "of the father") is nonetheless accented here once again, to hint that it was in the merit of Abraham ("father of a multitude of nations"—Genesis 17:5) that Lot's daughters conceived the seed of the Messiah. Abraham had been distressed by the revelation in the Covenant of the Parts that his descendants would suffer exile and enslavement (Genesis 15:13), and God had then promised that just as He would scatter them so would He gather them, and just as He would enslave them so would He redeem them. Ruth was the product of this promise to Abraham, as from her the house of David would arise, culminating in the Redeemer.

Boaz called her the "wife of Machlon" to indicate that had Kilyon's wife, Orpah, come, he would not have wed her.

And he declared thereby that his sole intention was to effect *yibum*, to perpetuate the name of the deceased.

According to the Zohar, the spirit of the deceased actually continues in the offspring of a levirate marriage, hence it is as if he himself is "raised up upon his inheritance."

4:11 וַיֹּאמְרוּ כָּל־הָעָם אֲשֶׁר־בַּשַּׁעַר וְהַזְּקֵנִים עֵדִים יִתֵּן יְהֹוָה אֶת־הָאִשָּׁה הַבָּאָה אֶל־בֵּיתֶךָ כְּרָחֵל וּכְלֵאָה אֲשֶׁר בָּנוּ שְׁתֵּיהֶם אֶת־בֵּית יִשְׂרָאֵל וַעֲשֵׂה־חַיִל בְּאֶפְרָתָה וּקְרָא־שֵׁם בְּבֵית לָחֶם:

All the people who were in the gate and the elders said, "Witnesses! May the Lord make the woman who is coming into your house be like Rachel and like Leah, both of whom built the house of Israel. May you prosper in Ephrata, and may your name be called in Bethlehem."

Although it is beneath the dignity of Israel's elders to serve as witnesses for ordinary transactions, it is fitting for them to be witnesses to a *mitzvah*, such as a marriage—particularly when the groom is the judge of Israel. The sages of the Sanhedrin therefore agreed to be "Witnesses!"

To dispel any qualms he might have had about marrying a woman of Moabite extraction who had gone against convention by pursuing him, the elders and the people assured Boaz that his new wife was like Rachel and Leah. They, too, came from idolatrous homes, which they abandoned to cleave to God. But her merit surpassed theirs, for they waited for Jacob to come to Laban's house and marry them, whereas she left her parents and came "into your house."

Moreover, in pursuing Boaz, Ruth followed the precedent of Leah, whose desire to build the house of Israel prompted her to go out and greet her husband saying, "To me shall you come" (Genesis 30:16). God considered this behavior so meritorious that He rewarded Leah with the birth of more tribes.

The assembled also praised the bride for possessing Rachel's beauty and Leah's modesty. And in keeping with the tradition that one who attends wedding festivities should bless the bride and groom and pray for them, the people prayed that she be beloved of her husband like Rachel, and like Leah bear him many sons; and that all her children be righteous.

No mention is made of the other matriarchs, because Hagar—whom Sarah gave Abraham in marriage, hoping "perhaps I will be built from her" (Genesis 16:2)—bore Ishmael, and Rebekah bore Esau. But all the children of Rachel and Leah—and all of the maidservants they gave Jacob in marriage in order to build the house of Israel—were righteous.

The elders mentioned Rachel before Leah. For just as Rachel had been barren and was later granted conception, so too Ruth, who had been barren during her ten-year marriage to Machlon, should now, at age forty, miraculously conceive.

[And just as Rachel and Leah "both . . . built the house of Israel," so would Ruth and Naomi together build the house of Boaz,] for Naomi would become nurse to the son born to him and Ruth.

It is noteworthy that the assembled Judeans, descendants of Leah, acknowledged Rachel to have been the mainstay of Jacob's home, and put her name before Leah's.

Having mentioned Rachel, who had died "on the way to Ephrata" (Genesis 35:19), they quickly added a blessing that Boaz "prosper in Ephrata."

In addition to wealth, which he deserved because he was not marrying for money, they wished him an abundance of children, since all the children from his first marriage had died. The *gematriya* of חַיִל is forty-eight, to hint of Jacob's thirty-four children [and grandchildren] from Leah, and fourteen from Rachel (cf. Genesis 46:8–15, 19–22).

They further blessed Boaz that he be like his ancestral kin Caleb, to whom Ephrata (Miriam) bore Chur, "firstborn of Ephrata and father of Bethlehem" (1 Chronicles 4:4).

According to a different interpretation, they said: "If you grow great in your immediate neighborhood of Ephrata, where your conduct and deeds undergo careful scrutiny, your fame will spread throughout the greater Bethlehem district."

In the merit of Boaz, the famine ceased, and he had saved Israel from their foes. So they prayed that from him should descend the king who would possess the strength (חַיִל) to vanquish Israel's enemies—as God later said to David, "Go engage in Torah study, and I will fight your battles"—and in whose merit Israel would become *bethlehem*, a house where bread was plentiful.

"May you raise a family of royalty like that of Peretz and establish the monarchy through this woman who took the initiative, as Lot's daughters and Tamar had done, and came into your house."

4:12 וִיהִי בֵיתְךָ כְּבֵית פֶּרֶץ אֲשֶׁר־יָלְדָה תָמָר לִיהוּדָה מִן־הַזֶּרַע אֲשֶׁר יִתֵּן יְהוָה לְךָ מִן־הַנַּעֲרָה הַזֹּאת:

"And may your house be like the house of Peretz whom Tamar bore to Judah, from the seed that the Lord will give you from this young woman."

Ever since Jacob said to Joseph, "In you shall Israel be blessed, saying, 'May the Lord make you like Ephraim and like Manasseh'" (Genesis 48:20), that has been the traditional Jewish blessing. However, since Boaz was a descendant of Peretz, the people blessed him that he build a house like that of his ancestor.

[Tamar, too, is mentioned here because of the parallels between her and Ruth.]

Just as Tamar dressed up and went to Judah, so did Ruth dress up and go to Boaz.

Just as Tamar did not bear children to her first husband Er or his brother Onan, who took her in levirate marriage, but to Judah, so Ruth did not bear children to Machlon or to his brother Kilyon, who took her in levirate marriage, but to Boaz.

When Tamar was giving birth, at first it seemed that Zerach would be firstborn and win the kingship of the house of David, but his twin brother Peretz pushed ahead and came into the world first, thereby becoming the ancestor of royalty. Similarly, when Ruth was being redeemed, at first it appeared that the other redeemer would establish the monarchy, but it turned out that the privilege went to Boaz.

Peretz and Zerach, was well as Ruth's son, were named by women. Because Tamar and Ruth acted for the sake of heaven, [they were graced with miraculous providence.] It was therefore fitting that their children be named by women, whose faith in God is stronger than men's, as evidenced by their refusal to participate in the sins of the Golden Calf and of the spies, and who are more sensitive to and appreciative of events that transcend the routine of nature.

4:13 וַיִּקַּח בֹּעַז אֶת־רוּת וַתְּהִי־לוֹ לְאִשָּׁה וַיָּבֹא אֵלֶיהָ וַיִּתֵּן יְהוָה לָהּ הֵרָיוֹן וַתֵּלֶד בֵּן:

So Boaz took Ruth, and she became his wife. He came to her, and the Lord gave her conception, and she bore a son.

The righteous Boaz kept his word to Ruth, who, significantly, is no longer called a Moabite. After buying the field in the presence of the elders and the people, he asked them to witness the marriage ceremony, and when they agreed and gave their blessings, he immediately married her.

The Jewish marriage ceremony consists of *kiddushin* (contracting the bond of "consecration" by, for example, the giving of a ring) and *nesuin* (the seven blessings recited under the *chupah*-canopy which make the couple legally man and wife.) Accordingly, the verse states that "Boaz took Ruth"—"taking" refers to acquiring by giving money or an object of value, i.e., *kiddushin*—and "she became his wife" (*nesuin*).

The field is not mentioned, for Boaz had no desire to actually acquire property. His only interest was in marrying Ruth to perpetuate the name of the deceased. Thus "Boaz took Ruth...."

Our sages elaborate: "She became his wife"—a worthy woman to a worthy man.

Just as "Boaz took Ruth" in joy for she was righteous and beautiful, so "she became his wife" with joy although he was very old, for her intentions were purely for the sake of heaven.

She did not need time to adjust to his opinions and wishes, but was immediately a wife to him.

Thus the brief marriage was perfect: "She became his wife," designated for him by heaven, as no other had been. That is why, although neither of them had surviving offspring from their previous marriages, together they two established a dynasty that will last as long as mankind.

"He came to her"—only after the wedding, as he had sworn to his evil inclination on the threshing floor.

Since the marriage was to fulfill God's will, and was consummated out of the purest motives, the scripture does not say, "she conceived and bore a son," but "the Lord gave her conception." Divine assistance was necessary because Boaz was very old and weak, and Ruth was a hitherto barren woman of forty. The miracle is ascribed to "her," however, because it came in the merit of her dedication in cleaving to Israel.

The *gematriya* of הֵרָיוֹן, "conception," is 271, the number of days of gestation. God arranged for her to give birth a full nine months after the wedding as a testimony that the child was conceived after the wedding and that the father was Boaz.

Indeed, everyone recognized that the child was blessed of God, and they therefore named him עוֹבֵד, Obed, that is, servant of God. According to an ancient Midrash, he was born circumcised.

Boaz is not mentioned again in the narrative, and the verse says only that she bore a son, not that she bore *him* a son, for he died that very night. This is further borne out by the fact that the child was named not by Boaz but by the women neighbors.

How quick must one be to perform a *mitzvah*! Had Boaz tarried but one day, the root of the house of David and the Messiah would not have come into being. This is in accordance with the verse, "Time to do for the Lord, they have violated your Torah" (Psalms 119:126). That is, those who defer doing a *mitzvah* by saying that there is yet time, in the end do not fulfill the Torah.

Thus the scripture says, "We are but of yesterday, and know nothing, for our days upon the earth are a shadow" (Job 8:9). That is, no one can be sure of today, for death can strike him down suddenly. One can count only days already passed. For man's days are like a shadow—not like the shadow of a tree or a house, but like the passing shadow of a bird flying by (Talmud).

According to the opinion that Boaz is Ibetzan, who had been punished with the loss of his many sons for failing to invite Manoach to their wedding festivities (Talmud, Baba Bathre 91a), he repented in his old age, and God forgave him and provided him with offspring to perpetuate his name. Had he however delayed one day, he would have died without an heir.

4:14 וַתֹּאמַרְנָה הַנָּשִׁים אֶל־נָעֳמִי בָּרוּךְ יְהֹוָה אֲשֶׁר לֹא הִשְׁבִּית לָךְ גֹּאֵל הַיּוֹם וְיִקָּרֵא שְׁמוֹ בְּיִשְׂרָאֵל:

The women said to Naomi, "Blessed be the Lord, Who has not left you without a redeemer this day. May his name be called in Israel."

The women knew that Ruth had previously had no womb and they immediately recognized the miracle in this birth and came to congratulate her.

At the same time, they came to comfort her and Naomi for the death of Boaz. "Blessed be the Lord" is an allusion to the customary words on such an occasion: "Blessed be the True Judge"—ברוך דין אמת.

The death of Boaz on the very night of their wedding ("this day"), they said, showed that only for this purpose had he come into the world. Although he had ended the famine through his prayer and conquered Israel's enemies, his major accomplishment was planting the seed of the house of David. Having done this, he went on to the light and bliss of eternal life.

Many strategems had been necessary to keep the Satan and the seventy angels of the nations from thwarting this act. But now that it had been done with the approval of the Sanhedrin, it could not be undone.

"Although you have not enjoyed long years together with your husband," they said, "thank God that you have been redeemed, and that the name of Boaz will be perpetuated through the son you have borne him."

Generations earlier, the patriarch Jacob, fearing that Joseph's descendants from the Egyptian convert Osnat would intermarry, had said, "May my name be called upon them" (Genesis 48:16), that is, may it be recognized that they are Israelites. Boaz, too, feared that his descendants from Ruth the Moabite might intermarry, and the women therefore said, "May his name be called in Israel"—may it be recognized that his seed is worthy of entering God's congregation.

They prayed that the newborn child become a great man like his father, whose name would constantly be on the lips of the people of Israel. They should heed his counsel and judgment, and they should name their children after him, for he would be a *tzaddik*.

The end letters of לך גואל היום, are the letters of מֶלֶךְ, king, to hint that just as Boaz had redeemed Ruth, so would their descendant redeem

Israel. And just as הַיּוֹם, "this day," [the sun] rules the sky, so would her seed rule Israel forever.

Generations later, when the queen mother Ataliah destroyed all the royal seed, one child—Yoash—escaped to continue the royal dynasty (2 Kings 11). And our sages declare that it was the women's blessing—"Who has not left you without a redeemer"—that saved David's seed from annihilation.

4:15   וְהָיָה לָךְ לְמֵשִׁיב נֶפֶשׁ וּלְכַלְכֵּל אֶת־שֵׂיבָתֵךְ כִּי כַלָּתֵךְ אֲשֶׁר־אֲהֵבָתֶךְ יְלָדַתּוּ אֲשֶׁר־הִיא טוֹבָה לָךְ מִשִּׁבְעָה בָּנִים׃

"And he shall be to you a restorer of life, and sustain your old age; for your daughter-in-law who loves you, who is better to you than seven sons, has borne him."

The new infant, said the women, would bring joy into Naomi's life and restore her spirit. And when he grew up, he would support her in her old age and bury her when she died. Furthermore, if she educated him to walk in righteousness before God, her soul would be rewarded in the World to Come for his good deeds, in accordance with the principle that "a son achieves merit for his parents" (Talmud).

Although his parents were Ruth and Boaz, they continued, the child could also be considered a son of Naomi, for the two women were of the same root. This is evident in the fact that, despite the natural antagonism between mother-in-law and daughter-in-law, Ruth loved Naomi to the extent of leaving her people to cleave to her, and she took better care of her than seven sons would have done.

Love of Naomi would therefore be in the child's blood. Just as the mother had picked in the fields to bring Naomi food, so would the son support her. And just as the mother had followed in Naomi's footsteps and learned from her to be good, so would the son.

According to a different interpretation, the women assured her that the child would be righteous because he was the product of seven generations of *tzaddikim* that preceded him: Peretz, Chetzron, Aminadav, Ram, Nachshon, Salmon, and Boaz. The seventh in line is saintly, and the eighth even more so, as hinted at by "who is better . . . than seven sons."

The women also hinted that the child would be the grandfather of

David, the youngest and best of Ishai's "seven sons" (1 Samuel 16:10); and he would be the tenth in line from Peretz, hence, most saintly.

The expression משיב נפש, soul-restorer literally, alludes as well to the resurrection of the dead that will take place during the reign of David's descendant, the Messiah.

4:16 וַתִּקַּח נָעֳמִי אֶת־הַיֶּלֶד וַתְּשִׁתֵהוּ בְחֵיקָהּ וַתְּהִי־לוֹ לְאֹמֶנֶת:

Naomi took the child, and placed him in her bosom, and became his nurse.

Unlike the noblewomen who leave their children in the care of servants and only occasionally handle and play with them, Naomi herself nursed, cared for, and played with this child. In addition, she guided him toward righteousness and educated him to serve God. Thus she nurtured him physically and spiritually, just as the women had predicted that he in turn would support her and bring merit to her soul.

There is an opinion that Naomi raised the child because Ruth died. However, according to our sages, Ruth lived to see the child's great-grandson Solomon sitting on the throne.

4:17 וַתִּקְרֶאנָה לוֹ הַשְּׁכֵנוֹת שֵׁם לֵאמֹר יֻלַּד־בֵּן לְנָעֳמִי וַתִּקְרֶאנָה שְׁמוֹ עוֹבֵד הוּא אֲבִי־יִשַׁי אֲבִי דָוִד:

The women neighbors called him a name, saying "There is born a son to Naomi." And they called his name Obed. He was the father of Ishai, the father of David.

The sudden death of Boaz on the night of the wedding had plunged Ruth and Naomi into grief. When the orphaned baby was born, they did not have the heart to name him, so the neighbors took matters into their own hands. At first they simply called him בן לנעמי, "a son to Naomi"; and only later, after he was weaned, did they name him Obed.

According to a different interpretation, Naomi and Ruth did not know whether the child should be named after Machlon or after the more recently deceased Boaz. They therefore called him Obed (עובד), "he who serves God," leaving the decision to Him Who knows men's souls and can best decide whose memory should be perpetuated.

The name Obed anticipates that he would learn Torah in order to fulfill its obligations and injunctions, and that he would engage in the "service of the heart" (*avodah*, עבודה)—prayer. Obed did both, and his progeny followed in his footsteps: "He was the father of Ishai" who "went out with a multitude [of disciples] and came with a multitude" (Talmud) and Ishai was the "father of David" who in the morning ruled on matters of Torah law, and at midnight rose to sing God's praises (Talmud).

"Let not the blessing of a simple person be light in your eyes!" our sages declare. For the blessing of the women—"May his name be called in Israel" (v. 14)—was fulfilled in Obed, who was renowned throughout Israel as a servant of God (עובד ה'); and as the father of Ishai, who died only because of Adam's sin, being himself sinless; and as the grandfather of David, "the sweet singer of Israel" and the fourth [after the patriarchs] to comprise the divine chariot [the "vehicle" through which God's name is made known to men].

Thus Torah never left this illustrious lineage, in accordance with the principle that if three successive generations are Torah scholars, the Torah will never be absent from their descendants, as it is written: "This is my covenant with them . . . My words that I have put in your mouth shall not depart from your mouth, or the mouth of your seed, or the mouth of your seed's seed . . . forever" (Isaiah 59:21).

"He was the father of Ishai, the father of David." It is for this statement that the book of Ruth was written, for its purpose is to record the lineage of King David.

It also comes to teach that one who seeks God with all his heart will succeed. Ruth strove with selfless dedication to cleave to Israel, and she merited to marry a leader in Israel and to produce David, to whom God promised the kingship as an eternal covenant.

4:18 וְאֵלֶּה תּוֹלְדוֹת פָּרֶץ פֶּרֶץ הוֹלִיד אֶת־חֶצְרוֹן:

And these are the generations of Peretz: Peretz begot Chetzron.

Having been told that Obed was Ishai's father and King David's grandfather, the scripture goes back in time to trace the lineage of Obed from Peretz, the ancestral father of monarchy.

It is a rule in scripture that the expression וְאֵלֶּה, "and these," adds to the previous matter. In this case, וְאֵלֶּה links the birth of Peretz to Judah and Tamar with the birth of Obed to Boaz and Ruth, to teach that both women acted for the sake of heaven.

Furthermore, just as the unusual events leading to the marriage of Boaz and Ruth were arranged by God to produce David, so were the unusual events leading to the union of Judah and Tamar, brought about by Him. [For the details of this incident see Genesis ch. 38.]

[Ruth merited to bear the royal seed because of her kindness and her devoted cleaving to God]. Tamar merited it because she was willing to suffer death, and with it the loss of the royal seed she knew she was carrying, rather than shame Judah. For she rightly perceived that even the highest purpose does not justify reprehensible actions.

According to the Midrash, the monarchy came through women of pagan origins so that the kings would have an element of cruelty from the mother's side, in addition to compassion from the father's side. This equipped them with the ability to exact revenge from Israel's enemies while treating Israel with compassion.

The three scriptural episodes leading to the emergence of David involved wondrous ways dependent on split-second timing; had the moment passed, they would have come to nothing. Lot's daughters sought to conceive from their father because they thought the entire world had been destroyed; had they waited, they would have discovered that it was not so. Judah was about to pass Tamar by and continue on his way when an angel impelled him toward her; and Boaz was about to die when he wed Ruth. All this comes to teach that as soon as the time is ripe, the Messiah will not delay in coming.

When Tamar was giving birth to her twin sons, Zerach put out his hand but drew it back, and Peretz was born first. "And she said, 'Wherefore have you made a breach (*peretz*) for yourself?' Therefore his name was called Peretz" (Genesis 38:29).

Our sages elaborate: Zerach wanted to come out first but God said, "The Messiah will descend from Peretz—shall Zerach come out first? Let him return to his mother's womb, so that Peretz will be first."

Peretz bore the seed of the monarchs, who break through to make way for themselves. Of his descendant the Messiah it is thus written: "The breaker (פּוֹרֵץ, *poretz*) shall go up before them; they shall break forth and pass on by the gate and go through it. Their king shall pass before them, and the Lord at their head" (Micah 2:13).

Peretz ("breach") alludes to the moon, which is sometimes

"breached" and sometimes "built"; Zerach ("radiance") alludes to the sun, which shines steadily. Zerach represents the priesthood; Peretz, the monarchy. Just as the moon grows to fullness in fifteen days, so did the monarchy grow to its full splendor in the fifteenth generation from Abraham to Solomon. David (דוד, numerically equivalent to 14), the fourteenth generation, is hinted at in the verse (Genesis 39:28): "When [Tamar] was giving birth, he gave a hand (יד, numerically equal to 14)."

Our sages say: All the דורות, "generations," in the scripture are incomplete (missing a letter *vav*), except for two: "These are the generations of heaven and earth" (Genesis 2:4), and "These are the generations of Peretz." The first describes the beginning of creation, before the angel of death came into being. At that time the generations were complete. After Adam and Eve sinned, God depleted all the generations in scripture. The generations of Peretz, however, are complete, because he was the forebear of the Messiah, in whose days God "shall swallow up death forever" (Isaiah 25:8).

In those days, the sun and moon [which was diminished for "complaining" that it and the sun were the same size, and "two kings cannot share the same crown" (Midrash)] will again shine forth with their original glory. And the light of the Messiah—which is now hidden because of our sins—will also shine forth in all its glory. The generations of heaven and earth, and the generations of Peretz, will be complete.

4:19, 20 וְחֶצְרוֹן הוֹלִיד אֶת־רָם וְרָם הוֹלִיד אֶת־עַמִּינָדָב: וְעַמִּינָדָב הוֹלִיד אֶת־נַחְשׁוֹן וְנַחְשׁוֹן הוֹלִיד אֶת־שַׂלְמָה:

And Chetzron begot Ram, and Ram begot Aminadav; and Aminadav begot Nachshon, and Nachshon begot Salmah.

Peretz generated a line of *tzaddikim* who each in turn begot another *tzaddik*. The fact that they were righteous is inferred from the doubling of their names, which shows that they had a double existence: they lived in this world and continue to live in the next.

Their virtues are hinted at in their names. For example, שַׂלְמָה, Salmah, whose name means "garment," was so called because he clothed [his soul] in a beautiful garment of good deeds. It was his namesake, Salmah the Righteous, who cancelled the watches placed by the king of the Israelite kingdom, Jereboam [to prevent his subjects from making their pilgrimage to the Holy Temple in Jerusalem, lest they be won over by the king of Judah (1 Kings 12)].

The name Salmah is derived from סֻלָם, *sulam*, ladder, and has the same letters as שְׁלֹמֹה, *Shlomo*, Solomon. Thus the Midrash says: Until Salmah they made ladders for *nessiim* (princes), henceforth for kings. That is, the generations from Peretz to Nachshon [leader of the tribe of Judah during the Exodus] ascended one degree after another until they merited kingship. The following generations again ascended in merit until they reached the "top of the ladder" in the person of Solomon, who reigned over both heavenly and earthly beings.

4:21 וְשַׂלְמוֹן הוֹלִיד אֶת־בֹּעַז וּבֹעַז הוֹלִיד אֶת־עוֹבֵד:

And Salmon begot Boaz, and Boaz begot Obed.

[Salmon is a variation of Salmah, mentioned in the previous verse.]

Boaz saved Israel from famine and foe, and he was stronger than a king, for of a king it is written, "He shall *give* strength to his king" (I Samuel 2:10) but Boaz personified strength (בּוֹ־עֹז, in him there is strength). He was also called Ibetzan (אִבְצָן), meaning father of the sheep (אָב לַצֹּאן, *av le'tzon*), for he was a shepherd of his people.

This book contains eighty-five verses, corresponding to the numerical value of בֹּעַז, Boaz. All except eight begin with the letter *vav*, for this Megillah was written for Israel, which circumcises its infants at the age of eight days.

Obed, however, was born circumcised.

Obed (servant of God) served God with all his heart, thereby fulfilling God's essential demand of a king. As David said, "And you, Solomon my son, know the God of your father and serve Him with a whole heart and a willing mind, for the Lord searches all hearts and understands the imaginations of all thoughts. If you seek Him, He will be found by you, but if you forsake Him, He will cast you off forever" (1 Chronicles 28:9).

4:22 וְעֹבֵד הוֹלִיד אֶת־יִשָׁי וְיִשַׁי הוֹלִיד אֶת־דָּוִד:

And Obed begot Ishai, and Ishai begot David.

The name יִשַׁי, Ishai, stems from יֵשׁוּת, existence. For Ishai never sinned, and if Adam's sin had not brought the decree of death upon mankind, Ishai himself would still exist in this world. It is fitting that "Ishai begot David" and established the eternal dynasty of the house of David, which will culminate in the revoking of the death decree during the Messianic era; may it come speedily in our day.

In Praise of the Proselyte

Ruth suffered poverty and loneliness to cleave to God, and she gave Israel the house of David and the light of the Messiah. From her story we learn compassion and love for the proselyte who leaves his father and mother to shelter under the wings of the *Shechinah*.

Precious are the גֵּרִים, proselytes, for the patriarchs and prophets called themselves גֵּרִים, which also means strangers. Abraham said, "I am a stranger and sojourner with you" (Genesis 23:4); Isaac was called a stranger, as God said to him, "Sojourn (גּוּר) in this land" (Genesis 26:3); and the sons of Jacob said, "To sojourn (לָגוּר) in this land have we come" (Genesis 47:4). David said, "For I am a stranger with you, a sojourner, as were all my fathers" (Psalms 39:13); "I am a sojourner in the earth" (Psalms 119:19); "For we are strangers before You, and sojourners, as were all our fathers" (1 Chronicles 29:15).

Our sages compared the proselyte to the ewe that fled from the field and joined the shepherd's flock. The shepherd loved the new sheep more than all the rest, for the rest of his flock he had to pay for, but he acquired her without payment. Similarly, God performed many miracles and wonders for Israel before they accepted the Torah, but the convert accepts the Torah without first witnessing miracles.

God loves Israel and converts equally, and converts are equal to Jews in all matters. It is a positive precept to "Love therefore the stranger, for you were strangers in the land of Egypt" (Deuteronomy 10:19). Therefore we are also commanded: "A stranger shall you not afflict [by reminding him of his past]; neither shall you oppress him [by cheating him]" (Exodus 2:20).

Converts are as dear to God as the Sabbath. The Torah warns twenty-eight times to treat converts properly, the same number of times that it warns against desecrating the Sabbath and against worshipping idols.

Precious are converts; throughout the scriptures they are likened to

Israel. Israel is called עֲבָדִים, servants, and מְשָׁרְתִים, ministers, as it is written, "For unto Me the children of Israel are servants; they are My servants whom I brought forth out of the land of Egypt" (Leviticus 25:55); and "You shall be named the priest of the Lord; men shall call you ministers of our God" (Isaiah 61:6). Proselytes, too, are called servants and ministers, as it is written, "Also the aliens that join themselves to the Lord, to minister unto Him and to love the name of the Lord, to be His servants" (Isaiah 56:6).

Israel are beloved, as it is written, "I have loved you, said the Lord" (Malachi 1:2); and proselytes are beloved, as it is written, "He loves the stranger, in giving him bread and clothing" (Deuteronomy 10:18).

Rabbi Shimon bar Yochai said: He who loves God is beloved of Him, as it is written, "He loves the stranger."

Of the righteous of Israel it is written, "But they that love Him be as the sun when it goes forth in its might" (Judges 5:31). Who is greater, he who loves the king or he who is beloved of the king? Obviously the latter: everyone loves the king; fortunate is he whom the king loves.

Onkelos the proselyte asked Rabbi Eliezer, "Is the entire love God has for the proselyte in that he gives him bread and clothing?" Rabbi Eliezer replied, "Is that a small thing in your eyes? For this Jacob prayed, saying, 'If God ... will give me bread to eat and clothing to wear'" (Genesis 28:20). Onkelos then came before Rabbi Yehoshua, who appeased him, thus: "Bread is the Torah, as it is written, 'Wisdom ... calls ... Come, eat of the bread' (Proverbs 9:1-5). Clothing is Torah, as it is written, 'You have a mantle (שמלה), be you our ruler' (Isaiah 3:6). Moreover, a convert's daughter can marry a priest and bear priestly sons who eat the showbread and wear the priestly vestments, and they are entitled to *challah* (a portion of dough that must be separated from all bread baked) and the first-shearing of wool."

Both Israel and proselytes are joined to God by a covenant. Of Israel it is written: "And my covenant shall be in your flesh" (Genesis 17:13). And of the proselyte it is written: "Also the aliens, that join themselves to the Lord ... Every one that holds fast by My covenant" (Isaiah 56:6).

The expression רצון, acceptance, is found concerning both Israel and proselytes. Of Israel it is written, "that they may be accepted before the Lord" (Exodus 28:38). Of the converts it is written: "Their burnt offerings and their sacrifices shall be acceptable upon My altar" (Isaiah 56:7).

Both are guarded: "Behold, He Who guards Israel neither slumbers nor sleeps" (Psalms 121:4); and "The Lord guards the strangers" (Psalms 146:9).

Converts are included in the four groups who answer before God, as described in the verse: "One [the righteous] shall say, "I am the Lord's; and another [children of the wicked] shall call himself by the name of Jacob; and another [the penitent sinners] shall subscribe with his hand to the Lord; and he [the proselyte] shall surname himself by the name of Israel" (Isaiah 44:5).

Rabbi Eliezer said: Joining Israel through conversion is considered as doing a kindness for all of Israel, as Saul said to Yithro's descendants: "For you showed kindness to all the children of Israel when they came up out of Egypt"(1 Samuel 15:6). Can anyone possibly do kindness for an entire nation? But because he converted—as we learn from his words, "Blessed be the Lord, Who has delivered you out of the hand of the Egyptians.... Now I know that the Lord is greater than all gods" (Exodus 18:10-11)—it is considered as if he did kindness with them all.

Precious are the converts, for God adds to their names, as in the case of Yithro. His name was originally יֶתֶר, Yether, as it is written, "And he returned to Yether, his father-in-law" (Exodus 4:18); but after he converted, a letter was added to make it יִתְרוֹ, Yithro. This marks high attainment, as in the case of Abraham ("Neither shall your name any more be called אַבְרָם, Abram, but your name shall be אַבְרָהָם, Abraham" [Genesis 17:5]) and Joshua ("Moses called הוֹשֵׁעַ, Hosea the son of Nun, יְהוֹשֻׁעַ Joshua" [Numbers 13:16]). On the other hand, the wicked cause their name to be diminished, as in the case of the false prophet אֶחְאָב, Echav, of whom it is written, "The Lord make you like Tzidkiyah and like אָחָב, Echav" (Jeremiah 29:22).

A gentile who embraces Judaism is rewarded like a Jew who has toiled at the Torah all his life. Thus Moses said to Yithro, "Come with us, and we will do you good, for the Lord has spoken good concerning Israel" (Numbers 10:29); and while Joshua reserved the fertile lands of Jericho for the tribe (Benjamin) that would lose part of its land to the Temple, in the meantime (for 400 years) the land was given to the descendants of Yithro, who left it after Joshua's death in search of another scholar to teach them Torah, as it is written, "The children of the Kenite, Moses' father-in-law, went up out of the city of palm trees [Jericho]" (Judges 1:16). They found a teacher, Yabetz, and moved near him, as it is written, "And the families of tribal scribes who dwelt with

Yabetz: the Tiratites, the Shimatites, and the Sokatites. These are the Kenites that came of Chammat, the father of the house of Rechav" (1 Chronicles 2:55). They are called תִּרְעָתִים, Tiratites (from תרע, to sound), for they sounded their prayers; שִׁמְעָתִים, Shimatites (from שמע, to hear) for their prayers were heard; and שׂוּכָתִים, Sokatites (from שׂכה, to protect), for their merits protect Israel.

One of the Kenites, Yonadav ben Rechav, had heard a prophet foretell the destruction of the Temple, whereupon he ordered his sons not to drink wine, build homes, or plant vineyards. As his descendant was to recall, "We will not drink wine; for Yonadav the son of Rechav our father commanded us, saying: 'You shall drink no wine, neither you, nor your sons, forever; neither shall you build a house, nor sow seeds, nor plant vineyard, nor have any; but all your days you shall live in tents'" (Jeremiah 35:6,7). Because they obeyed the instructions of their father, "Therefore thus says the Lord of Hosts, God of Israel; There shall not be cut off unto Yonadav the son of Rechav a man to stand before Me forever" (Jeremiah 35:19).

Said Rabbi Yochanan: Greater is the covenant that God made with the sons of Yithro than that which he made with David, for the covenant with Yithro was unconditional, whereas the covenant with David was not. Thus it is written, "If the children forsake my law. . . . Then will I visit their transgression with the rod, and their iniquity with strokes" (Psalms 89:31–33); "but if your children keep My covenant and My testimony that I shall teach them, their children also forever shall sit upon the throne" (Psalms 132:12).

BIBLICAL QUOTATIONS

Genesis		6:13	9
2:18	118	7:11	98
12:1	76	9:3	42
12:3	102	12:29	99
12:10	15	17:4	9
15:13	129	18:10–11	143
16:2	130	18:13	127
17:5	129, 143	20:21	65
17:13	142	22:24	86
18:5	80	22:26	53
19:2	112	23:33	44
19:12	112	28:38	142
19:32	95		
23:4	141	Leviticus	
26:3	141	10:12	21
27:22	7	19:9–10	1, 8, 61, 70, 103
27:27	36	19:18	14
28:10	31	23:22	61, 70
28:30	142	25:5	70
29:21	101	25:55	142
30:16–17	101	Numbers	
33:14	12	10:29	143
35:19	130	13:16	143
36:12, 22	73	14:11	84
37:21–22	79	15:15	103
37:33	36		
38:1	14	Deuteronomy	
38:26	14	1:17	4
38:29	138	8:10	97
39:1	55	10:18	142
39:2	18	14:21	103
39:7	104	14:22	64
39:28	139	16:20	9
42:36	27	23:4	73, 77
47:7	141	23:7	v, 13, 14
48:16	135	24:1	77
49:10	4	24:19	70, 82
		25:5	40
Exodus		25:7	13
2:4	17	28:3	65
2:20	141	28:40	81
3:5	81	32:18	43
3:6	4		
4:18	143	Joshua	
4:27	79	5:15	125

[145]

Index

Judges		44:5	143
1:16	143	56:6, 7	142
2:15	8	57:2	36
2:17	5	58:7	85
3:12	7	59:21	137
3:18	vii	61:6	142
3:31, 4:1	7		
4:21	6	Jeremiah	
5:6	7	20:6	26
5:31	142	29:22	143
6:12	65	32:41	53
12:8	57	35:6, 7	144
16:3	99	35:19	144
16:23	98	51:59	39
17:15			
19, 20	15	Ezekiel	
		14:21	6
1 Samuel			
2:10	140	Hosea	
8:5	12	5:5	53
15:6	143		
24:5	98	Joel	
25:31	77	2:18	31
25:44	99		
		Micha	
2 Samuel		2:13	138
3:27	125	5:1	50
7:18	80	7:8	34
21:16, 22	25, 43		
23:15	15	Zechariah	
24	97	9:9	
1 Kings		Malachi	
2:19	75, 92	1:2	142
5:18, 19	92		
19:13	98	Psalms	
		27:4	75
2 Kings		39:13	141
4	64	40:8	vi
11	135	41:2	22
20:5	v	72:17	106
20, 21	72	78:70–72	14
		89:30–33	144
Isaiah		103:20	54
3:6	142	112:9	11
9:15	4	113:9	37
11:3, 4	4	119:62	99
25:8	139	119:126	134

121:4	143	2:7	61
132:12	144	3:7	1
133:3	47	4:2	8
146:9	143	4:3	59
147:14	6	4:7	8
		4:9	59
		4:10	23

Proverbs
9:1	144	4:11, 12	vii
9:5	6	4:17	vi
13:25	97	4:18	vi
15:27	57		
19:17	75	Lamentations	
22:9	85	2:15	50
22:23	23	3:22	50
24:5	57		
24:23, 24	4	Ecclesiastes	
27:4	75	11:5	51
29:25	102		
31:10	91	Esther	
31:12	20	1:10	98, 106
31:17	107		
31:23	19	Daniel	
31:26	91	11:44	51
31:27	84		
		Ezra	

Job
5:10	10	2	11
8:9	134	8:26	75
17:19	49		
22:28	111	1 Chronicles	
31:32	40	2:19	17
1:1	1	2:55	144
1:2	20	4:4	130
1:6	32	4:22	16
1:7	32	22:9, 10	37
1:8	vi, 24, 38	28:9	140
1:9	39, 43	29:15	141
1:20	26		
1:21	21, 52	2 Chronicles	
1:22	54	2:1	67